The Small Business Perseverance Guide

Small businesses are the largest contributors to net, new jobs in America. They drive innovation, generate employment, and promote community development in a constantly changing environment. These vital enterprises fuel our economy and strengthen the social fabric of our communities. Yet, they often face steep challenges that test their fortitude, flexibility, and ultimately, their perseverance.

For small business owners navigating the turbulent waters of entrepreneurship, this book is a strategic guide. It was written with the clear understanding that owning and growing a small business is not for the faint of heart. Each day brings new hurdles—whether it's adapting to shifting market trends, managing unpredictable cash flow, staying ahead of technology, or weathering global disruptions like pandemics and economic downturns. Through all of this, the pressure to make the right decisions never lets up, and the margin for error can be incredibly small.

This book is the result of the author's direct experiences working alongside small business owners across a wide range of industries. It distills years of insight into the practical realities of running a business when the stakes are high and resources are limited. The advice contained within is not theoretical—it is grounded in real-life situations and tailored to help small businesses survive, adapt, and thrive. You'll find proven frameworks, margin-focused strategies, and examples that illustrate the path from chaos to clarity.

At the heart of this guide is the belief that perseverance, coupled with a strategic mindset, can turn even the toughest challenges into stepping stones for growth. It's about thinking critically, making intentional choices, and understanding the numbers behind your decisions. Strategy isn't just for big corporations—it's the key to small business resilience.

The small business journey is unpredictable, but it is also incredibly rewarding. This book will help you unlock that potential by teaching you how to strengthen your financial foundation, identify margin opportunities, build systems for scalability, and lead with confidence. Whether you're trying to stabilize your operations, accelerate profitable growth, or simply regain control of your business, this book is here to serve as a roadmap. Success in small business isn't just possible—it's within reach. Let's get to work.

The Small Business Perseverance Guide

How to Make Money and Prosper During Challenging Times

Manny Skevofilax

Routledge
Taylor & Francis Group

NEW YORK AND LONDON

Designed cover image: Shutterstock

First published 2026
by Routledge
605 Third Avenue, New York, NY 10158

and by Routledge
4 Park Square, Milton Park, Abingdon, Oxon, OX14 4RN

Routledge is an imprint of the Taylor & Francis Group, an informa business

ISBN: 9781041018421 (hbk)
ISBN: 9781041018438 (pbk)
ISBN: 9781003616597 (ebk)

DOI: 10.4324/9781003616597

Typeset in Garamond
by Newgen Publishing UK

Dedication

This book is dedicated to the memory of my Mother and Father, who immigrated to America from the island of Karpathos, and gave me the opportunity to pursue the American Dream.

Contents

Acknowledgments

Special thanks to you, Dr. Alan Weiss, for your encouragement. I am grateful for your mentorship. This book would not have been possible without you.

About the Author

Manny Skevofilax is a consultant, speaker, and author who helps business owners maximize profits and overcome growth challenges to achieve financial freedom. An expert in strategic planning, financial statement analysis, and business operations, he's been achieving extraordinary outcomes for his clients since 2003.

A Baltimore, Maryland native, Manny earned a Bachelor of Science in Business and a Master of Science in Finance from the Merrick School of Business at The University of Baltimore.

Prior to starting his career as a consultant, Manny's background includes formal bank credit training and service as a Vice President with Comerica Bank, a U.S.-based commercial lending institution. He has corporate lending experience in the continental U.S. and European markets, with specialties in commercial business finance, real estate finance, and large corporate syndicated lending for mergers and acquisitions.

Manny grew up in the restaurant business and made a career change to corporate banking at age 29. When he's not helping business owners, Manny can be found exploring the ancient ruins on the island of Karpathos where his parents were born.

Introduction

Perseverance: *The continued effort to do or achieve something despite difficulties, failure, or opposition.*

Small businesses are the largest contributors to net new jobs in America. They drive innovation, generate jobs, and promote community development in a constantly changing environment. These important entities face great difficulties that test their fortitude, flexibility, and ultimately, their perseverance. *The Small Business Perseverance Guide: How to Make Money and Prosper During Challenging Times* is a strategic guide to help small business owners navigate the turbulent waters of the business world.

This book is the result of my experiences with the challenges faced by small businesses, including shifting market trends, unstable financial conditions, and the emergence of international catastrophes like pandemics and economic downturns. It is designed to work as a guide for small business owners, providing useful tips, creative solutions, and real-world examples to uplift and direct you through your darkest moments.

According to the U.S. Bureau of Labor Statistics (BLS), approximately 20% of new businesses fail during the first two years of being open, 45% during the first 5 years, and 65% during the first 10 years. Only 25% of new businesses make it to 15 years or more. These statistics haven't changed much over time and have been fairly consistent since the 1990s.[1,2]

For example, why does a restaurant on one corner succeed and the one on the other corner fail? Believe it or not, it's not the food!

At the heart of this guide is the belief that perseverance, coupled with a strategic approach, can transform challenges into opportunities for growth and success. A small business's journey is full of unknowns, but it's also full of potential. This book aims to unlock that potential by guiding you through the process of fortifying your business against the odds,

DOI: 10.4324/9781003616597-1

by identifying and seizing opportunities for growth, and by building a sustainable and profitable business model that thrives in challenging times.

The chapters within are purposely designed to be read in any order. You will find chapters that cover some of the most essential topics that small businesses need to master in challenging times, including the importance of a resilient business model, practical strategies for managing financial health, adapting to changing market conditions, leveraging technology and innovation, and maintaining customer relationships.

As you turn the pages of *The Small Business Perseverance Guide*, you'll discover that the key to thriving during challenging times lies not in avoiding obstacles but in embracing them. With each challenge comes an opportunity to learn, grow, and redefine what success means for your business. This book equips you with the knowledge, tools, and mindset needed to navigate the complexities of the business world, ensuring that your small business not only survives but prospers.

Whether you're a seasoned entrepreneur or at the helm of a startup, this book offers valuable insights into making informed decisions, optimizing operations, and driving your business forward. This book is more than just a collection of strategies; it's a testament to the power of perseverance. The path of entrepreneurship is never easy, but it can be rewarding for those who dare to persevere.

Welcome to a journey of resilience, growth, and success. Welcome to *The Small Business Perseverance Guide: How to Make Money and Prosper During Challenging Times*.

Notes

1 www.investopedia.com/financial-edge/1010/top-6-reasons-new-businesses-fail.aspx
2 U.S. Bureau of Labor Statistics. "Table 7. Survival of Private Sector Establishments by Opening Year."

Chapter 1

Understanding the Landscape

Market Overview of Economic Factors. How Did We Get Here? Interest Rates, Losses, Reduced Sales, Too Many Expenses

The US economy is cyclical in nature. Downturns are followed by recoveries, which are followed by downturns. Nothing continues to go up without coming down, unless you achieve escape velocity in leaving the Earth's gravity. But the market isn't a spaceship. So we must be prepared for both dynamics, exploiting "ups" and mitigating "downs."

Consumer behavior also shifts—with price sensitivity, normative pressures, advertising, economic fears, and so forth. This can lead to temporarily reduced sales or to the forced abandonment of certain products and services being offered. Not only did the market for buggy whips drop dramatically, but so did that for cassette players, high-sugar-content foods, and movie theaters. Technology, health concerns, keeping up with the neighbors, and even boredom can accelerate these changes in tastes and perceived needs.

Remember Blackberries? (Not the Fruit!)

More recently we've become sensitized to supply chain disruptions—accidental (a ship lodged in the Suez Canal), internationally deliberate (attacks on Red Sea shipping), and nationally deliberate (the

DOI: 10.4324/9781003616597-2

Longshoreman's Union port strike). Many organizations are trying to create shorter, more controlled, and more secure supply chains for themselves.

PERSEVERANCE PRESSURE

As this is being written, the US is considering building (or reopening) nuclear plants, but since a great deal of uranium fuel has come from Russia in the past, the country is trying to find sources within its borders or its allies' borders.

How safe is your supply chain? How safe are potential supply chains you may need in the future, as in those nuclear plants and uranium fuel needs?

During volatile times, access to traditional financing may change or even disappear. Standards for credit may tighten and new factors might be introduced into credit scores. It's vital to maintain a strong credit profile, collection of receivables, and to never have overdue accounts payable.

We've also witnessed a great deal of regulatory change and government "safety net" changes. Thus, it's not only important to stay out of trouble spots, it's also important to be a top candidate for government programs, such as the PPP[1] initiatives during the COVID-19 pandemic. It's vital to stay informed and compliant, but also to take advantage of whatever is being offered.

Economic volatility leads to increased competition in many sectors, as businesses expand, contract, and/or pivot into new ventures. Yesterday's brand may not be tomorrow's. Famed coach Marshal Goldsmith points this out in his book, *What Got You Here Won't Get You There*.[2] Competition, counterintuitively and not understood by enough business owners, *broadens markets* rather than narrows them. Burger King builds stores across the street from McDonald's because they know people are showing up in the area for burgers. (And you can make a case, in terms of pivots, that fast-food companies are more in the real estate business than the food business.)

Many small businesses have survived tough economic times (such as the pandemic) by moving exclusively into remote sales and/or *raising* their prices. You can make a case that DoorDash and Uber Eats are products of turning bad times into good times for business. IBM was once known for business machines, then software, and now consulting (from where most of its profits come today). Amazon started as a book distribution business.

Markets that manifest true need—and not fads—invite innovation and new approaches for new profits. People will pay for smart TVs or laundry delivered to their homes, but not for new cases for pet rocks.

All of this, of course, accepts the inevitable role of technological progress in all aspects of business. The pushback against it can be severe, as well. A two-day strike of dockworkers in 2024 sent the capital markets plummeting. Not unlike the Luddites of the industrial revolution, workers were protesting the potential loss of jobs due to automation, AI, and other forms of technological progress. (And unlike General Ned Ludd, Harold Daggett, the current head of the International Longshoreman's Association, makes nearly a million dollars a year, drives a Bentley, and lives in a 7,000 square-foot-home in a tony New Jersey suburb. He recently sold his yacht.[3])

While inflation can be low, consumer prices can still be high, especially for essentials such as mortgages, fuel, food, insurance, and so forth. Technological advances can help offset this, but not if we have persistent resistance. In "understanding the landscape," we have to realize that the landscape often shifts beneath our feet! And as with quicksand, the more we panic and struggle, the more quickly we drown. That means we need to remain calm, and to have contingency plans, commonly known as "Plan B" and "Plan C," and so on down the line.

People often believe they're far worse off than they actually are, which leads to conservatism in investing and spending. Many is the restaurant which hasn't changed its excellent food nor its reasonable prices, but which customers feel they "can't afford to dine in anymore."

Technology plays a key role, of course, in adapting to changing market conditions and even *creating them*. E-commerce and remote work are obvious and ubiquitous examples, but personal medical portals, online customer "chat" opportunities, and advanced inventory efficiencies are also creating huge advantages.

PERSEVERANCE PRESSURE

While using the proper technology in the right manner for your business can save you enormous amounts of money, using the improper technology in the wrong manner may cost you your business altogether.

We are not "replacing ourselves" in the West, meaning morbidity is outpacing fertility. There will not be enough people for either "white collar" or "blue collar" labor in the next decade unless we make intelligent use of immigration, extended contributions from people beyond "normal" retirement age, and artificial intelligence.[4] So the question becomes not "if" but "how" your business will accommodate this significant demographic change *in both your employees and your customers.*

We could easily see rising costs (securing the right talent, technology, and so forth) and lower demand (seniors don't require another house, a college education, or more cars). It's quite probable that advanced degrees—and even college degrees—will be less in demand outside of specialties (such as medicine or law) as people hire for competence and not credentials.

Interest rates and inflation will continue to cause market turmoil and impact buying decisions. One of the difficulties with the housing market is that even if interest rates decline by two points, for example, seniors living in homes with 3% and lower mortgage interest rates are not going to "downsize" to smaller homes with 6% interest rates. They will stay where they are. Hence, the inventory of new homes declines and, therefore, prices increase. This affects builders, designers, contractors, furniture, insurance, lawn care, and so on.

Takeaway

The variety of economic factors above should impress upon you that a comprehensive understanding of the economic landscape is an unassailable asset. If you don't personally have the ability or the interest, you'll need advisors who can provide it: a board, attorney, accountant, consultant, and so forth. Some of these factors cannot be prevented, but you can be prepared to deal with them if and when they do occur. Others, such as AI and demographic change, are occurring as you're reading this.

No matter how "tough" or tumultuous the economic times may be, there are always opportunities if you know how to navigate them. In the next section, we'll examine trends and perceptual shifts that will provide the tools and insights to help you prepare for the continuing volatility of the marketplace.

Understanding Market Trends and Consumer Shifts

Keeping abreast of market trends and consumer behavior shifts helps businesses make informed decisions. This ensures that strategies are aligned with the current economic environment. Market trends can be driven by rational reactions to the Fed's interest rates, or competitive imports, or mergers, or innovation.

But they can also be driven by normative pressure and even "irrational" reactions. "Hot" new restaurants are jammed for a month, but then empty-out when people grow tired of them and move on to newer, hotter restaurants. Tesla's space-age new pickup truck garnered a great deal of attention and early orders, but then was seen as rather hideous in person, impractical, hard to keep clean, and even potentially dangerous because of all the sharp angles!

Consumer shifts are similarly affected by temporary pressures. People put political signs on their lawns, but then they disappear. A fashion craze dies out because everyone begins to look the same. (Inexplicably, wearing a baseball cap backwards has stayed with us.) A heavily-advertised discount will clear excess inventory off a car dealership's lot, but that groundswell disappears when the discount ends.

Of course, some changes are more permanent. The pandemic required remote meetings and interactions. And in its wake, now years later, the convention and conference businesses are considerably less than pre-pandemic. It's turned out that meeting remotely is quite adequate without the great expense. Similarly, air travel and lodgings have increasingly been the result of vacation and recreational travel, and far less business travel. You can meet online, but you can't be in a theme park (though you no longer need to be present in a casino to gamble).

By understanding changes in the market, businesses can identify new opportunities for growth. Some examples include untapped niches or emerging consumer needs.

Since airlines are so hard to contact by phone and often charge more for tickets booked by phone, apps have been developed to allow customers to find what schedules exist on which routes and to book flights from their mobile devices. Some banks have put in coffee bars. DoorDash and Uber Eats cater to people seeking take-out dining who don't want to take a trip to the restaurants. (And packaging has been created to keep food hot during the delivery delay.)

People are increasingly comfortable with remote communications, so companies have produced high-quality mics and specialized lighting for Zoom calls, as well as the ability to use different camera angles. Pickleball has taken over (often forcing tennis courts to convert) and created a marketplace for pickleball clothing, accessories, and equipment—even medical responses to middle-aged people who aren't as spry as they think they are.

PERSEVERANCE PRESSURE

New opportunities for growth and niche markets reward those who are there first. It's better to be there imperfectly and "course-correct" than to be the perfect response but the 49th one in the market. Loyalty most often accrues to those providing immediate gratification.

Awareness of market trends enables businesses to position themselves competitively. Those who can differentiate their offerings are able to capitalize on their unique value proposition. Some trends at this writing (which may well change by the time you are reading this):

- Take-out dining from even higher-end restaurants
- "If not now, when?" attitude about investing in vacations
- Reliance on trusted others' recommendations (referrals)
- Online ordering of everything from clothing to office equipment
- Increasing numbers of remote workers and productivity concerns
- Reluctance to embrace all-electric vehicles
- Reverse migration to the northern US due to climatic disasters
- Sweeping generational demographic changes

Merely considering that last bullet point should give you cause to pause. The Baby Boomers and GenX cohorts have occupied most of the top positions in business, academia, and politics since about 1993. That is all radically changing, and new tastes, norms, and beliefs are becoming apparent in commerce. In addition, the tens of trillions of dollars in intergenerational wealth transfer—spawned by the Reagan-era IRA legislation—have created huge shifts in financial power, and will continue to do so for at least the rest of this decade.

These trends, which may affect businesses generally or be more specific to certain businesses (e.g., construction, consumer goods, insurance) lead us to consider what is traditionally known as "risk management."

Understanding market trends helps in anticipating potential challenges and planning accordingly. This reduces the impact of market fluctuations on business operations.

Risk management is about two essential planning elements:

■ Seeking to prevent the likelihood (likely causes) of events occurring which are detrimental to business (or personal) success. Posting "no smoking signs" and separating combustible materials are likely to diminish the probability of fire.
■ Seeking to mitigate the adverse effects of a problem should it occur, such as sprinkler systems and insurance policies to diminish the consequence when a fire does happen.

No risk management efforts can be successful without both considerations, since we may be unsuccessful in preventing a likely cause (someone smokes carelessly anyway, despite the signs) or we haven't anticipated all likely causes (arson). But note that no matter how effective the contingent actions (no matter how good the sprinklers), we will have experiences of loss of money, time, repute, and, perhaps, life.

We've used a simple example of "fire" to make this point. But apply the principles to your financing, health benefits, retirement plans, staffing, safety, regulatory compliance, and so forth and you'll find that what we so easily call "risk management" is essential in detail and attention for any understanding and management of changing market trends and conditions.

Insight into consumer and market trends ensures that resources are allocated efficiently. This helps business owners to focus on areas with the highest potential for return. The emphasis here is on "insight."

Your experiential intelligence from starting and running your business is often more valuable and accurate than any number of surveys, polls, or predictions. Trust your own judgment, based on your customers/clients, location, history, and relationships. No financial or sports prognosticator has ever been fired or held accountable for the inaccuracy of his or her predictions and recommendations.

And never forget: *No one* predicted the internet.

By aligning offerings with current market demands, businesses can drive revenue growth, even in challenging economic times. There are some products and services that have to be ended or suspended; some that have to be adjusted or improved; and some that have to be replaced. Almost everything has a "shelf life" in business, even customer relationships.

Takeaway
Understanding market trends and consumer shifts is not just about surviving challenging times, but also about positioning your business

for success in the future. It's about being proactive and responsive and ensuring your business remains relevant and competitive. What can be more important than that?

Impact of Global Events on Local Economies (A Few of the Basics)

Global economic trends, such as trade tensions or international market shifts, can have a localized impact on businesses. They can affect local demand for products and services. There are the positives, such as a great deal of American culture sweeping the world in the form of clothing (Nike), celebrity (Taylor Swift)[5], technology (Apple), and other business trends and fads.

The negative aspects of this are best represented by supply chain problems, from the boat mistakenly grounded in the Suez Canal, to the car carrier that caught fire and sank with $400 million in vehicles on board,[6] to the people attacking cargo ships in the Red Sea. These positive and negative global events have affected a huge range of companies, large and small. *And they have prompted companies to reduce the length of their supply chains, better protect them, create alternatives if they're disrupted, and, ultimately, try to keep them close to home.*

The pandemic, of course, created huge volatility and required businesses to be agile and resilient. One of the key lessons learned was that businesses (and individuals) who had liquid, available cash fared far better than those who did not. That spiked investments and savings which, when the perceived threat was passed, resulted in huge expenditures of vacations, travel, and consumer goods.

PERSEVERANCE PRESSURE

The overused phrase about "global economies" has finally proved to be true. No business owner or senior executive can afford to simply read the local newspapers and listen to the local affiliate's newsreader on TV and assume they're sufficiently educated about events that can promote or threaten their business.

The uncertainty caused by global events can lead to shifts in investment, with investors either pulling out of markets perceived as risky or investing in markets seen as safe havens. This can impact local businesses and economies far beyond the actions of local management.

Venture capitalists and private equity firms have a huge impact on a global scale. Chrysler is owned by Stellantis, headquartered in Amsterdam. During the Brexit crisis and later vote in the UK, a great deal of London's financial powers fled to Paris, Amsterdam, and Zurich. Independent films ("indies") are being made all over the world and competing in traditional award events. The most popular beer in America at the moment is Modelo, which is brewed in Mexico.

VIGNETTE

The Biden government placed a premium on electric cars and urged a near-total switch to them in the very short term. Yet the same government placed a 100% tariff on very good Chinese vehicles which, at about $40,000, would be available to the middle class, because the party in power did not want to threaten the automotive union votes in the approaching election. And they may not get those votes anyway. Such are the complications of global events.

Global events can lead to volatility in currency markets which can impact the cost of imports and exports for local economies. This can affect pricing, profitability, and economic stability at the local level. Here's an example of the euro-to-dollar fluctuations over the past five years, as an example: In the last five years the euro has ranged from $1.10 up to $1.23, down to $.96 and at this writing is $1.08. That's a range of 27 cents on the dollar. You can see how that would impact imports, exports, fees for long-term projects or deliveries, borrowing, and so forth.

Surprisingly, these fluctuations aren't necessarily correlated to wars, supply chain breakdowns, natural disasters, technology breakthroughs, or new competition! They are subject to normative pressures, perceived threats and opportunities, rumors, political actions, and innate biases.

Nvidia, based in California but a global company, saw its sky-high stock fall dramatically in 2024. Boeing, one of only two major airframe makers in the world, has seen its stock drop by about 50% over the past five years.

If this can happen to huge enterprises, it can happen to small businesses which are inextricably linked to the global economy.

The pandemic underscored that "cash is king" in terms of resiliency and survival. Cash can be easily lost, however, if the wrong decisions are made in times of fluctuations and volatility.

Here are some guidelines for money management in volatile times:

- **Invest in your strengths.** If you have to cut back, do so elsewhere. We've seen hotels that cut expenses "in the background" unknown to guests and unfelt by guests. But some reduce their amenities, or bell staff, or spa hours which can prevent even loyal patrons from returning.
- **Don't cash in your investments unless you desperately need more cash.** Talk to your financial planner first. Don't lose on the downside and then miss the upside.
- **Rigorously pursue receivables.** Many businesses still bill months after services are performed. The longer you wait to collect money, the less your money is worth! Look at it this way: If you don't assertively follow up on overdue payments, you're cheating every one of your customers or clients who is paying on time.
- **Create strong relationships with your bankers.** Provide them with enough business (checking accounts, savings accounts, mortgages, loans, investments, and so forth) that you're seen as an important customer who deserves the best treatment. (Remember the old cliché: If you borrow $100,000 you're a customer. If you borrow a million dollars you're a partner!)

For local economies reliant on tourism, global events such as pandemics or geopolitical tensions can lead to a significant downturn in visitor numbers. This can affect local businesses and employment.

A cargo ship knocked down the Francis Scott Key Bridge in Baltimore, Maryland, costing local businesses about $15 million per day. The ironically-named Ever Given was the ship stuck in the Suez Canal, disrupting supply chains globally, with an estimated $54 billion in losses as a result. Note that a) both of these events have been blamed on human error; and b) local businesses globally were harshly affected—missing inventory replacement, delaying new orders, and having to pay underutilized staff members.

When the Felicity Ace sank with all those luxury autos, businesses that served auto distributors, repair shops, financing, insurance, and other products and services suffered, and those firms did not have the insurance that the auto makers or dealers carried, and couldn't afford to lodge what would be low-probability-of-success lawsuits.

Tourism has enjoyed a huge boost with the decline of COVID, but has a great deal of ground to make up for pandemic-incurred losses. Hotels are still understaffed in most cases, and airlines are still recovering. United Airlines has only recently reported (October, 2024) that it was able to restart a share repurchase program that had been suspended since 2020 due to the COVID pandemic.[7]

The way local governments respond to global events, through fiscal policies, subsidies, or restrictions, can significantly impact local economies. These responses can influence business operations and consumer behavior.

The Biden Administration had placed a high priority on supporting the transformation to electric vehicles. The costs in so doing are astronomical and the impact on a great deal of the economy formidable.

We've earlier alluded to the impact of the government's hypocrisy in placing huge tariffs on these vehicles, effectively keeping them out of the US economy. How can small businesses predict and/or react to such events out of their control? This is even worse in election years, where the winners may or may not adhere to campaign promises and formidably impact the economy and, perhaps, undermine small business strategies.

Local government can have the same influence. Are liquor licenses granted or denied? Are local taxes increased? Are new regulatory laws helpful or harmful. (Examples: number of parking spaces required by restaurants; parking limits in commercial areas; restrictions on deliveries; permits for Uber and Lyft; changes in zoning laws; creation of affordable housing requirements of builders; evening curfews.)

In response to global challenges, there can be an acceleration in the adoption of new technologies. New technologies can transform local economies and create new opportunities for businesses and workers.

The problem, of course, is how to use technology for profitable growth and not merely for its own sake. The "high tech, high touch" of John Naisbitt of *Megatrends*[8] of over 40 years ago is absolutely accurate today. Just watch customers trying to use automated checkout registers in pharmacies and supermarkets, where employees have to be available to help them with the confusing procedures, and you'll realize that not all technology improves speed and efficiency!

We might enjoy automated service reminders for our cars or lawns, but not the lack of humans to explain what's needed and why, justify the charges, and make recommendations to us for the future.

Global events as well as national and even local events can lead to inflationary pressures in local economies which can affect the cost of living and purchasing power of consumers. This can impact consumer spending and economic growth.

Takeaway

Global events have far-reaching impacts on local economies, influencing everything from consumer behavior to supply chains to government policies. Understanding these impacts is crucial for businesses that are trying to navigate these challenges effectively. Don't believe that a small business can afford to "think small" or merely locally.

Understand the "landscape" within which you operate and will be operating. *If that sounds daunting, consider the consequences if you fail to do so!*

Notes

1 Paycheck Protection Program https://en.wikipedia.org/wiki/Paycheck_Pro
   tection_Program#:~:text=The%20Paycheck%20Protection%20Program%20all
   ows,applicant's%20average%20monthly%20payroll%20costs.
2 See *What Got You Here Won't Get You There*, Marshall Goldsmith,
   Hyperion, 2007.
3 www.newsweek.com/harold-daggett-salary-trump-connection-us-port-strike-
   1962260
4 The Bureau of Labor Statistics estimates that as soon as 2030 there may be more
   people over 60 in the US than there are children, which is unprecedented.
5 The French reported that Taylor Swift's contribution to the French economy
   when she appeared at the Eiffel Tower in concert was greater than that of the
   entire Olympic Games. People from the US went to Paris and Warsaw to see
   her, because it was cheaper, including the air fare and lodging, than to purchase
   tickets for the US tour.
6 https://programbusiness.com/news/cargo-ship-carrying-thousands-luxury-
   cars-sinks-atlantic/#:~:text=Experts%20in%20incident%20insurance%20Russ
   ell,%24155%20million%2C%20according%20to%20Russell.
7 https://ir.united.com/static-files/e8f60718-632e-4794-a60d-69cb2264af37#:~:text=
   CHICAGO%2C%20Oct.%2015%2C%202024,%2Dtax%20margin1%20of%209.7%25.
8 *Megatrends*, John Warner, Warner Books, 1982.

Chapter 2

Building a Resilient Business Model

Understanding Business Model Resilience

Understanding how to craft a resilient business model helps businesses adapt more quickly and efficiently to changes. The ability to adapt quickly ensures long-term sustainability. Let's define two aspects:

Resilience: The ability to "bounce forward" from setbacks. Resilience is not about gracefully accepting defeat or setbacks and living to fight another day. It's about *learning in the moment* and moving forward from the obstacle. A resilient army does not retreat; it forges ahead. You can lose a battle but win the war.[1]

Likely Changes: We are facing today continuing change in areas that include:

- Technology
- Demographics
- Supply Chain Reliability
- Education
- Natural Disasters
- Social Justice

DOI: 10.4324/9781003616597-3

- Climate Concerns
- Public Safety
- Terrorism
- Health and Medicine
- Immigration Concerns
- Generational Traits

Hence, adaptability in the face of such change and the need to bounce forward is a key contributor to profitable growth. No one predicted the internet or the 2020 pandemic. There was great suffering, but at this writing, in the US, there is a great recovery.

A resilient business model incorporates strategies for identifying, assessing, and managing risks. These strategies can minimize the impact of unforeseen events or crises on operations and revenue.

No matter how well we prepare, some risks and their consequences can't be avoided. We've seen what hurricanes, tornadoes, wildfires, and flooding can do, no matter how we try to prepare. In our businesses, despite all precautions, a competitor may develop a superior technology, excellent clients may leave for unpreventable reasons (e.g., the sale of their business), and we may be unable to replace veteran, talented workers because replacements aren't to be found within economic compensation levels.

The organizations that best survived and even prospered during the pandemic were innovative and managed risks well. They had cash on hand, easily moved to remote marketing and implementation, kept loyal customers satisfied, and held on to important employees and assets.

By consistently meeting customer needs, even in adverse conditions, businesses can build and maintain strong customer loyalty, which is invaluable for long-term success.

Loyal customers will always give you the "benefit of the doubt" in questionable circumstances (Was the delivery on time?) or even errors (The product wasn't ready as promised). It's a good idea to "triage" your customers periodically into these categories:

1) **High value:** Frequent purchases without regard to price or asking for "deals." No returns requested. Provide referrals without being asked. Suggestions and ideas for additional products and services.

2) **Moderate value:** Periodic purchases. Respond better to discounts; returns are infrequent. Will provide referrals if asked. May "price shop" at other providers.

3) **Low value:** Infrequent purchases. Always request discount or bonuses of some kind. Do not provide referrals or respond to surveys unless unhappy. Actively complain about pricing.

Develop and sustain category 1 and provide special favors for this group. Respond readily to category 2 and consider over time whether they should move up to category 1 or down to 3. For category 3, provide no special deals and refuse demands and unreasonable requests. If they are costing you more than they're worth (e.g., dresses are returned with perspiration stains from use), let them go and take them off your mailing lists.

Companies that demonstrate resilience often have a clear mission and adaptability that engage employees, leading to higher retention rates and a more motivated workforce. Just make sure you're retaining the best customers and not the worst (see above)! You will need to reach out to customers and never take the good ones for granted. We've found attorneys who never bother to contact clients about will updates, despite ten years having passed and families and net worth having changed. That's a recipe for ending relationships and referral sources.

PERSEVERANCE PRESSURE

With prospects, you won't be successful without trust. And with customers, you'll be undermined if you lose that trust.

Businesses that successfully navigate crises with minimal disruption enhance their reputation with customers, suppliers, and partners. This helps businesses build trust and credibility. The classic case was Johnson & Johnson pulling Tylenol off the shelves when someone tampered with random products. More recently, McDonald's pulled its quarter-pounder burgers in affected states when *E. coli* was discovered in the slivered onions from one of its suppliers.[2]

On a more "local" basis, however, there's the difference between an auto dealership disputing a scratch on a recently purchased new car, vs. another fixing it for free without question. There's the painter who returns to fix an uneven finish instead of claiming it was weather-related. And, of course, the restaurant that removes an unhappy customer's meal and provides a new one without question or charge.

A resilient business model protects against downside risk. It also positions the business to capitalize on new opportunities for growth as they arise, ensuring the business remains relevant and prosperous. On a large scale, we've seen Netflix as a provider of rented DVDs raise prices and lose 600,000 customers virtually overnight, then switch to a streaming service that is ridiculously successful artistically, winning scores of industry awards, and financially, expected to be about $43 billion in revenue in 2025.[3]

On a smaller scale, during the pandemic, many businesses closed brick & mortar stores and became solely internet retailers. Others realized that their value was even greater when people couldn't easily leave the house *and consequently raised their prices.* Others collaborated with companies such as DoorDash and Uber Eats to provide home delivery of pharmaceuticals, gifts, flowers, and all kinds of food (we knew about pizza delivery, but Chinese spareribs, pasta carbonara, and hot dogs?).

Resilience requires that you trust your judgment so that you make better decisions and also recover from bad decisions rapidly. Some people see an error and consider it defeat. But some consider it a learning experience.

Thus, business model resilience is really the combination of a general resilience in your life, because the trait is not turned "on and off." Make "unconscious competency" your default position. And just in case you doubt that's possible, think of the times that you:

- Took a different route in your car when faced with a traffic jam
- Changed flights when you were late for your original connection
- Changed sources when your supplier didn't live up to promises
- Adjusted your day because of unanticipated family needs
- Changed a work procedure that failed to work for you

Finally, as we've mentioned repeatedly, understanding and planning for resilience includes developing a robust supply chain that can withstand various disruptions. This ensures continuous operation and product delivery. By "robust" we mean secure, short, and stable.[4]

Takeaways

Focusing on building a resilient business model is essential for navigating the complexities of the modern business landscape. It ensures that a

*business can withstand shocks, adapt to changes, and emerge stronger.
This helps to secure its place in the market for the long term. And let's not
forget that disruption, volatility, and turmoil can be very effective, offensive
market techniques that can lead to strong brands and dominance.*

Flexibility in Business Operations

The US economy is cyclical in nature. Downturns are often followed by
periods of recovery. It's important to be prepared for both phases. Nothing
goes up without going down at some point, but in the longer term, the US
economy has trended reliably upwards.

When we talk about flexibility, we're talking about being proactive.
You might say that resiliency kicks in *reactively* after facing a setback. But
flexibility is meant to create the conditions where you are successful despite
economic shifts, or even *because of them.* As we've mentioned before,
people and organizations who had cash did far better surviving and even
thriving during the pandemic, *because the cash gave them greater flexibility*
in changing their business models.

What worked well yesterday may not work well tomorrow, which is why
gas stations are now mini-marts where many customers show up and don't
even purchase gas!

Economic challenges can lead to dramatic shifts in consumer behavior.
Some examples include increased price sensitivity and changes in
purchasing priorities. Sometimes, certain purchases are completely
discontinued. Do-It-Yourself (DIY) can flourish during hard times and boost
the revenues of a Home Depot, Lowe's, and the local hardware store.

Post-pandemic, we're experiencing a huge rise in tourism, which offsets
the drop in business travel, and boosts the hospitality industry (while
hurting the conference and events industry).

Let's revisit supply chains in the name of flexibility. Global and local
economic challenges, wars, natural disasters, and other events can
disrupt supply chains. This can adversely impact costs and affect business
operations. It's important to have flexible and resilient supply chain
strategies in place for such possibilities.

You may want to consider:

- More than one supply chain source from different origins
- Supply chain safety as part of your strategy and senior meetings

- Shortening the chain and trying to make it regional or even local
- Providing the key elements yourself if possible

And don't overlook the fact that information and intelligence about the market and your competition is part of your supply chain.

PERSEVERANCE PRESSURE

Financing is easy to obtain in good times when it isn't really needed, but difficult to obtain in tough times when it is needed drastically. Create a solid liquid financial reserve.

Small businesses may face challenges in securing financing during tough times, including tighter lending standards. Therefore, it's important to try to always maintain a strong credit profile. Consider every loan you take, how quickly you pay it off, the receivables and payables that are overdue, and any other factor that can affect your business and personal credit score. Then improve it.[5]

Pay local bills first, if you have to set priorities. American Express isn't going to cancel your card if you're a week delayed in paying your bill, but small businesses are extremely dependent on cash flow *as you well know!* So treat them as you'd like to be treated.

Government policies and support programs can change in response to economic conditions and/or who is in power at the moment. It's important to stay informed and compliant. During the pandemic, companies profited through government assistance programs, but it was important to keep careful records to avoid payback requirements by proving that the money was used in compliance with government restrictions.

Economic downturns can lead to increased competition in certain sectors as businesses pivot or diversify to find new revenue streams. It's important to have strategies that make your business stand out. These strategies can't be developed in the midst of desperation or new competition. They must be in place now, created during stability, and ready to be implemented if needed. (For example, if you anticipate refocusing on remote sales, have the technology in place, the people trained, and the promotional material completed.)

Don't be caught "flat-footed" when confronting radical changes. We've stated before that as a simple example, organizations (and individuals) with substantial amounts of cash fare far better during turbulent times no matter what the causes of the turbulence.

Technology plays a role in adapting to changing market conditions, including the adoption of e-commerce and remote work tools. A large consideration, of course, will be artificial intelligence. The unalterable fact is that in most of the developed world and especially the US, morbidity is outpacing fertility, and we will have fewer workers over at least the next two generations. One of the three ways to deal with this is through what we used to call "automation" and now call "technology" with emphasis on AI.[6]

An important consideration is the suitability of technology for your operation. It doesn't work or help if not oriented toward your particular situation. (Just look at the people assigned to help with grocery self-checkout, at machines designed to be used automatically by customers.) The "high touch" aspect can't be omitted from the "high tech" aspect. We see this done successfully on websites which allow customers to conduct live "chats" with employees (and not "bots"). Amazon, the master of technology, has had people call me about problems. If they can do it, so can you.

Technological innovation can be intimidating if we assume (or are led to believe) that it's *mandatory* for our growth. No customer ever told me they were overjoyed to talk to my voice mail.

Challenging economic times can affect the labor markets. Some effects include changes in employment rates and the availability of skilled workers. Also, upward wage pressures play a significant role in being able to afford hires.

Let's take a moment to focus on the labor and customer dimensions of significant demographic change, with an aging population living longer and fewer young people (children and grandchildren) in the population:

- What is now "child care" will decline and "elder care" will grow.
- Theme parks and amusement areas will decline.
- Streaming services will increase, movie theaters will decline.
- Clothing will shift to an emphasis on older people, comfort, and flexibility.
- More home aids (chairs on stairs, recliners) will be sought.
- Organizations may need to offer facilities for pets, elder care, health and personal grooming, exercise, and shuttle services.
- Fewer cars may be on the roads, especially at night. Drivers and autonomous cars will expand in popularity.

- Schools will close.
- Income tax revenues will decline.
- Social security will be threatened not by politicians, but by its faulty underlying math.

PERSEVERANCE PRESSURE

The time to prepare for demographic changes is now. *Don't try to hire replacement workers when the workforce has already shrunk. Don't shift your product lines after the original customers have long since departed.*

Interest rates and inflation can have a big impact on business operations. Some effects are rising costs and reduced consumer demand. You can't predict interest rate and inflation rises and falls, of course, but you can be prepared for them. Look to refinance when interest rates decline. Have cash ready if and when inflation grows.

"Cement" long-term customers who will remain loyal to you no matter what the economic times or your prices. Create alternate suppliers who may be able to give you better deals or replace failed suppliers. If possible, avoid borrowing in times of high inflation. Stress your highest-margin items. Consider introducing new products and services that appeal more to the changing demographics discussed earlier.

Takeaway

It is important that business owners possess a comprehensive understanding of the economic landscape. These important points will equip them with the knowledge to navigate challenges and seize opportunities during all economic times.

Scalability for Sustainable Growth

Scalability allows a business to expand its operations and reach without incurring proportional increases in costs. This enables more efficient growth. "Scalability" is the ability to be changed in size and "heft." The easiest example is businesses which use the internet and can reach expanding geographies and markets without any increase in overhead or physical plant or property.

Compare that to a "brick & mortar" operation which must build new outlets (e.g., McDonald's or Starbuck's). This is a "crisis" area for colleges, which are increasingly turning to online options, especially in light of high tuition costs needed to fund those new buildings.

How can you scale your business? Give some thought to:

- Dedicated "take-out" options (food)
- Have the customer come to you (rental cars)
- Combine multiple services (clinics with many specialists and equipment)
- Cross training (have salespeople who can sell *all* your products and services)
- "One-stop contact" (a "360° banker" who is the single contact for the customer)

Increasing scalability (and not undermining it) should be a key criteria for any new initiative and for all strategy considerations. For example, plan to merge or partner with a company that enhances your scalability, and doesn't decrease it. A scalable business model provides the flexibility to adapt to market changes and customer demands quickly. This ensures the business remains competitive and relevant.

By managing costs effectively as the business grows, scalability can lead to higher profit margins. The ability to grow revenue faster than expenses is crucial for long-term sustainability. *Investors are more likely to fund businesses with scalable models because they offer a clearer path to significant returns on investment.* A scalable business model demonstrates potential for substantial growth.

Ultimately, scalability is about ensuring the long-term viability of a business. It prepares the business to face future challenges, seize opportunities, and sustain growth over time.

Takeaways

Focusing on scalability from the outset can position a business for sustainable growth. Scalability enables a business to navigate the ups and downs of the market. It also helps a business to continuously meet or exceed customer expectations.

A truly scalable business will both increase current profitability and long-term business valuation. The business will be much more attractive to prospective buyers and/or for succeeding family members who will run the business. Today, with remote means, achieving scalability is "easier" than ever, but it nonetheless requires a dedicated effort to achieve it.

At this writing, Amazon has introduced tele-health service charged by the appointment, including prescriptions sent to a pharmacy, for between $29 and $49.

Adopting a Customer-Centric Approach

A customer-centric approach prioritizes the needs and preferences of customers leading to higher satisfaction levels. Satisfied customers are more likely to become repeat buyers and advocates for your brand. Isn't it amazing how many businesses seem to operate as if the enterprise would be wonderful if customers simply didn't get in the way?!

- The grouchy coffee shop worker at 6 am.
- The flight attendants who feel they're *not* there for service, which is 90% of the job.
- The security person who feels everyone is guilty until proved innocent.
- The medical office receptionists who feel no need to return calls promptly.

PERSEVERANCE PRESSURE

Every organization has customers (clients, or members, or students, etc.) and it can't exist without their continuing patronage. An insurance company can do business without insurance agents, but not without people who are seeking insurance.

By consistently meeting or exceeding customer expectations, businesses can foster loyalty. Loyal customers are less price-sensitive, more forgiving of mistakes, and more likely to refer others. The only thing worse than having no trust is having trust and losing it. Loyal customers will always give you the "benefit of the doubt" when you have the inevitable error, mistake, or screw-up. They don't expect perfection or immediate access, but they will demand apologies and rapid responsiveness.

Happy customers are more likely to share their positive experiences with friends, family, and social networks. They act as powerful advocates for your brand and help to drive organic growth. *Most executive purchasing decisions are made on the basis of peer-to-peer referral—not the internet, advertising, or any other means.*[7] Consequently, delighted customers will share the word to help their colleagues and also to "get credit" for suggesting good sources, such as you.[8]

A customer-centric approach involves understanding individual customer needs and preferences. It allows businesses to tailor their offerings and communications which leads to more personalized and engaging customer experiences. Thus, you have a built-in "laboratory" to test new ideas, products, and services. You'll have real-time "experts" who can tell you if your website is helpful or not, and what they'd like to see in the future.

Never allow your operation to become employee-centric. Employees should be treated well, of course, *but not at the expense of customers.* Employees should answer the phones at 5 pm and not be packed up and ready to leave at 4:45pm. Remember: If an employee is a problem, it's the fault of management.

By listening to customer feedback and understanding their evolving needs, businesses can develop or improve products and services that truly solve customer problems and fill market gaps. This ranges from physical layout to high tech vs. high touch, from hours of operation to variety of offerings.

Other factors for customer-centrism include:

- **Increased Revenue:** Customer-centric businesses often see higher revenue growth due to increased customer loyalty and word-of-mouth referrals. Happy customers are also more likely to purchase additional products or services.
- **Enhanced Crisis Resilience:** During tough times, a loyal customer base can be a lifeline. Businesses that have built strong relationships with their customers are more likely to weather economic downturns and other crises.
- **Informed Strategic Decision-Making:** A customer-centric approach ensures that strategic decisions are made with the customer's best interest in mind. It aligns product development, marketing, and sales strategies with customer needs and expectations.

Takeaways

Adopting a customer-centric approach contributes to immediate business success and lays the foundation for long-term resilience and adaptability. It ensures that the business remains relevant and competitive in a rapidly-changing market.

Let's turn now to the financial management that must underlie and support all of this.

Notes

1 In fact. Ulysses S. Grant won the Civil War for the Union by departing from his predecessors and continuing to move south, even when temporarily defeated by Robert E. Lee. He learned from such setbacks and his troops' morale was greatly enhanced by moving forward instead of backward.
2 https://corporate.mcdonalds.com/corpmcd/our-stories/article/always-putting-food-safety-first.html.
3 www.cnbc.com/2025/01/21/netflix-nflx-earnings-q4-2024.html
4 Of course, true resilience would suggest a backup supply chain, as well!
5 Sometimes merely applying for a credit card or cancelling one can hurt your credit score.
6 The other two are the use of an intelligent immigration policy and the continued use of the wisdom of "seniors" by abandoning artificially low retirement mandatory ages (which will also mitigate the current math dooming the Social Security system).
7 See for example, *Invisible Influence,* Jonah Berger, Simon & Schuster, 2017.
8 About 70% of happy customers will share an experience with at least six other people: www.superoffice.com/blog/customer-experience-statistics/

Chapter 3

Financial Management in Challenging Times

This chapter will equip readers with the knowledge and tools necessary for making informed financial decisions. These financial decisions are important because they lead to stability and growth even in the most challenging economic climates. The chapter is for readers looking for actionable tips to navigate their companies through challenging economic times.

Prioritizing Expenses

Essential Needs First: Prioritize expenses that are essential for survival and well-being, such as housing, utilities, groceries, and healthcare. These should always be at the top of your list. Note that these should be both personal and professional. Insurance, for example, for you, personally, includes:

- Life
- Auto
- Property
- Health
- Umbrella
- Theft
- Disability[1]
- Disaster (flood, earthquake)
- Custom (collections and hobbies)

In your business you'll need insurance tailored for your needs. If you have employees, you'll need to cover them to some extent as well. These needs might include theft, customer lawsuits, harassment, illegal termination,

DOI: 10.4324/9781003616597-4

travel, product malfunction, workers compensation, and so forth. If you have health insurance, your employees get it too!

Debt Obligations: Make minimum payments on all debts to avoid penalties, fees, and damage to your credit score. If possible, focus on paying down high-interest debts first.

Be aware that every time a bank or other organization so much as investigates your credit—whether or not you actually do business with them in any way—your score is adversely affected. This is also the case if you apply for a new credit card offer, *whether or not you are accepted, or if you pay off and close a credit card account!*

It's a good idea to check your credit scores weekly to both understand how your actions and habits are affecting your scores *and to see if any mistakes or unauthorized use are affecting you.* You can do so with software such as WalletHub.com. Also, there are three major credit bureaus in the US—Equifax, Experian, and TransUnion—which may or may not show equal results for you. *You can't be sure which one is being used by your bank or auto dealer until you ask.*

Beyond that, make sure you pay off your bills promptly—entire balances if possible, but at least more than the minimum due. Pay off local businesses first, which need the money more than giant companies and which you need for your local supplies and services. Exchange debt sources when possible to lower your interest rates and to present a much better credit risk. "Reduce and refinance" should be your mantra for improving your credit score health.

Insurance Premiums: Keep up with insurance payments, such as health, home, and auto insurance. Insurance provides a safety net against significant financial losses. I've mentioned types of personal and professional insurance needs earlier. You are best served by an independent broker who is not employed by an insurance company, but who can sell many types and brands of coverage for the best deals.

Never consider insurance as an investment. Term life insurance, with no accruing cash value, is an excellent alternative for inexpensive coverage. Review your insurance with your broker at least twice a year to determine changes needed because of:

■ Family additions
■ More (or fewer) employees
■ Term policies expiring
■ New property

- Changed laws and regulations
- Additional growth risks (travel, investments, etc.)
- New belongings

Non-Essential Expenses: Review and reduce spending on non-essential items and services. This includes dining out, entertainment, subscriptions, and luxury items. I'm not suggesting you have a "poverty mentality," which is actually disadvantageous. But you may find that you're doing things "out of habit" that no longer justify the expense.

As an example, many people have magazines piling up on their real or virtual desk that they intend to "get around to," but never do. The question to ask is, "If I never read any of these, will it hurt me?" After all, if they were important, wouldn't you make it a priority to read them before now?!

Negotiate and Shop Around: Regularly review and negotiate recurring expenses like phone bills, insurance premiums, and utility services. Shopping around can also help you find better deals. It may behoove you to have someone do this for you. For example, the plethora of phone, internet, and cable TV charges can be overwhelming. Assign an assistant (or hire a temporary one) to point out to you economies of scale, duplications, and unnecessary charges (especially on your credit cards).

You'll find local stores will give you discounts for constant business. Even the chains (e.g., Staples) provide discounts for "members" and loyal customers. Your local printer or graphics artist may give you a break in return for payment in advance or cash (formally reported, not under-the-table).

Focusing all your charges on, say, an American Express Platinum Card will also generate points you can use for travel (personally or professionally), automatic upgrades on check-in when available, early check-in and late checkout options—even being met and escorted through airport immigration and customs on international tips. Amex provides detailed billing and appeals procedures, as well as merchant accounts with which you can use customers' credit cards for payment.

Try not to spread charges over different credit card providers, so as to maximize your "clout" with one of them. The same holds true, of course, for your banking needs. If you place your mortgage(s), business loans, personal loans, investments, and bank accounts at the same institution, you will have much more leverage than if you deal on a lesser scale with four separate banks. You will also be able to seek a "personal banker," one person to contact for any concern who would be able to find you the help you need, rather than you having to take the time to do so.

PERSEVERANCE PRESSURE

It's said that if you borrow $100,000 from a bank you're a customer, but if you borrow $1 million you're a partner! Focus on a single bank "partner" and meet the high-ranking officers to expedite your needs in the future and be a "known" entity in the bank.

Plan for Future Expenses: Set aside money for upcoming known expenses, such as annual insurance premiums, car maintenance, or property taxes. Planning ahead can prevent these costs from becoming financial burdens. You can use "auto-pay" to automatically send money from your business or personal accounts: Simply make sure that you always have a sufficient balance. This is why it's always a good idea to get overdraft protection for your accounts, in case you misjudge. Be sure to repay it as soon as possible. Also, make certain that your accounts are FDIC (Federal Deposit Insurance Corporation)-insured.

You'll also need to fund for *unknown* future expenses not covered by insurance or other means. That may mean a new technology, replacing unexpected employee departures, repairing or replacing equipment failures, and vehicle breakdowns.

Takeaway
By carefully prioritizing your expenses, you can navigate challenging financial times more effectively, ensuring that your most important financial obligations and goals are addressed first. Money is not a resource, it's a priority.

Monitor Cash Flow Closely

Use financial software to leverage and help you track your cash flow in real time. These tools often offer insights and analytics to better understand your financial patterns. There's a variety of software products available to help with cash flow at any given time.

Monitoring cash flow is important because you'll learn if the plans we've discussed thus far (e.g., anticipating expenses and providing for unexpected expenses) are accurate and sufficient. You can also quickly determine if cash flow is below expectations and search for the cause, which may be eminently correctable. However, you have to be aware of the problem first. Like a boat taking on water, there comes a time when no amount of bailing can save it.

Monitoring cash flow can help you determine:

■ If you're suffering from theft
■ If there are distinctions among sales sites or employees
■ If your products and services are affected by new competition or technology
■ If your offerings are aging and not contemporary
■ If your constituency and demographics have changed adversely

And of course, this can help you take advantage of such conditions before it's too late.

Perform cash flow analysis regularly to assess the health of your finances. This involves comparing projected cash flows to actual cash flows and investigating any variances.

Keep your financial records up to date by recording all transactions as they occur. This habit ensures that your cash flow analysis is always based on the most current information. Your accountants can tell you whether "cash" or "accrual" methods of accounting are best for you, but you need to be current in any case with your records.

Items of importance:

■ Loan payments due
■ Credit scores
■ Expense vs. plan
■ Insurance claims pending
■ Overdraft and loan amounts
■ Cash on hand
■ Income vs. plan
■ Travel expenses
■ Legal cost pending
■ Interest and dividend income

Of special and most important note here are *accounts receivable*. If your business involves billing clients, keep closely focused on accounts receivable. Follow up on outstanding invoices promptly to ensure that cash inflows remain steady.

This is a critical problem for small businesses. The ownership—the top people—do not regard overdue invoices as a high priority. They seem content that the invoices were sent, which of course is irrelevant if they're not paid on time! And the emphasis is *on time*.

The longer you have to wait for a payment, the less your money is worth!

Consider some of these options to collect your money quickly and without spending more money in order to collect it!

- Offer a small discount (5%) for full payment in advance.
- Limit returns to one week, and consider offering credits, not refunds.
- Never invoice for payment "on completion."
- Consider invoicing for "due on acceptance," even far ahead of delivery.
- Otherwise, payment should be "due on presentation of our invoice," never "net 30" or beyond.

When you give people 30 days, they take 60. Always insist on immediate or even advance payment. The old "late fees will be 1.5% of the total" is a worthless threat. No one is actually hurried by it, and you won't be able to collect it in any case.

When a customer or client is overdue, immediately contact them the next day. (Some organizations actually "ping" people a week before, alerting them that a payment date is approaching. Even such established firms as American Express and AT&T do that monthly.)

Sometimes your invoice isn't received or lost, but other times the customer might be having cash flow problems. In the worst case, work out a payment plan, but remember that if your customers aren't managing their businesses well, that doesn't mean you should adopt that bad habit.

For businesses that hold inventory, optimize inventory levels to avoid tying up too much cash in stock. Use inventory management techniques to balance having enough stock to meet demand without overinvesting. This might seem obvious, but it's often hard to accomplish.

Cancelled orders, discounted options to increase inventory from suppliers, and overly-optimistic sales forecasts can all result in excess inventory. It seems that we can read daily about auto dealerships complaining to the manufacturers about having to accept too many vehicles at too high a price. At least those cars can be resold. You can't resell stale bread or out-of-style clothing.

Use any of the very helpful inventory tracking software packages available (just Google the phrase and you'll find scores of options and reviews). But also make sure your staff is diligent in creating the proper input for the software.

Of course, in many businesses, the major problem with inventory control is seasonal fluctuations, so be prepared.

If your cash flow is subject to seasonal variations, plan for these fluctuations in advance. Save excess cash during peak seasons to cover expenses during slower periods. Of course, sometimes you alter products and services by season; more so in the North. The lawn experts of the spring and summer become the leave and debris-cleaners of the fall and the snow-plowers of the winter. The more sophisticated pool companies don't lay people off in the fall, but instead refocus them on equipment repairs and future sales.

Establish specific cash flow targets for different periods (weekly, monthly, quarterly) and monitor your performance against these goals. Adjust your strategies as needed to meet these targets.

The retail business is a prime example of a cash flow high wire act. They generally expect 75 percent of income to be generated in the fourth quarter, and 75 percent of that in December during the holiday season. Some arts groups plan for a huge annual event—such as *The Nutcracker* for ballet, and *A Christmas Carol* for regional theaters—that supports the remainder of their season. This leaves them exposed to such problems as inclement weather closing the doors or a rival production opening within commuting distance.

Cash flow should also be examined in terms of earned and unearned income. For charities and nonprofits in general, when earned income (ticket and product sales, known as "merch" these days) is higher than unearned income (donations and grants), there's usually good cause to be alarmed. We refer to this phenomenon as being "upside down." It's extremely difficult to support these endeavors without strong donor support (which requires very little expense and overhead to generate) and even "patrons" who can fund huge campaigns or seasons.

The time to take action about cash flow shortages is *immediately*, so that you are able to compensate with special sales, fundraisers, cutting expenses, reducing programs, and so forth (as well as responsibly using credit lines and debt).

Let's emphasize that the people and organizations that did the best—survived and even thrived—during the pandemic were those with cash: sufficient cash not only for daily needs, but also to take care of emergencies *and invest in opportunities.*

Thus, it's vital to maintain and build a cash reserve. Aim to build and maintain a reserve that can cover several months of operating expenses, at a minimum. A year would be optimal. This reserve can be crucial for weathering periods of negative cash flow. And it can accommodate unexpected expenses, such as repairs, insurance claim denials, legal issues, employee departures, and modernization of software.

Further, having a reserve provides the ability to take advantage of disruptive times by acquiring new office space, purchasing a competitor's inventory, creating remote purchasing options, and so forth. Cash is more than "king," it's the ace.

Takeaway

By implementing these strategies, you can gain a deeper understanding of your cash flow, allowing you to make informed decisions and take proactive steps to maintain financial stability during challenging times. What many people don't appreciate is that this isn't solely protection, it's also about opportunity.

You can't raise the amount in the pot unless you have the chips to play with.

Negotiate with Creditors and Suppliers: Start Here

Before entering any negotiation, gather all relevant financial information, including cash flow analyses, current and projected financial statements, and any documentation of financial hardship. Being well-prepared will strengthen your position. Creditors are far better off with a slower payment scheme than with no payment scheme. But pay close attention to the aforementioned credit score and try never to be overdue or in default.

Reach out to creditors and suppliers early, before financial issues become critical. Proactive communication demonstrates your commitment to finding a solution and maintaining a positive relationship. Be transparent and share your financial situation honestly, including any ongoing challenges and your efforts to address them. Transparency builds trust and can lead to more sympathetic consideration from creditors and suppliers.

PERSEVERANCE PRESSURE

Don't try to fool creditors, it's too easy to find one's credit report and score. Be honest, because others have been in your situation and can empathize. But if you make commitments, always meet them.

Understand Creditors' Positions: Allowing you leeway isn't a sign of weakness nor an invitation to continue to be overdue. It's a business gesture to help you both, so honor it in that regard. Research and understand the needs and constraints of your creditors and suppliers. Knowing their priorities can help you propose solutions that are beneficial to both parties.

Present a clear plan outlining how you intend to meet your obligations. This could include revised payment terms, partial payments, or extended deadlines. A concrete plan shows that you are serious about resolving the situation. You can also request reduced interest rates or fees. If dealing with debt, ask if creditors can lower interest rates or waive late fees. Reducing these costs can make it easier for you to catch up on payments.

Seek Payment Extensions or Deferrals: For both creditors and suppliers, inquire about the possibility of extending payment deadlines or deferring payments. This can provide you with the breathing room needed to stabilize your financial situation.

Remember, even the IRS will agree to Payment Terms on Overdue Taxes!

Propose Trade-offs: Consider offering something in return for concessions from creditors or suppliers. This could include longer-term contracts, future bulk orders, or other incentives that might appeal to them. (Airlines and hotels have been known to offer free flights and rooms, for example.)

Above all, maintain professionalism and courtesy. Always approach negotiations with professionalism and respect. Maintaining a positive relationship is crucial for long-term cooperation and support. Document your agreements. Ensure that any agreements reached are documented in writing. This protects both parties and clarifies the terms of the agreement, including any new payment schedules or conditions.

Takeaway

By employing these strategies, you can more effectively negotiate with creditors and suppliers. These strategies can potentially secure terms that help you navigate through challenging financial periods while preserving important business relationships.

Adopt a Flexible Budgeting Approach

Understand Variable vs. Fixed Costs. Differentiate between fixed and variable costs in your budget. This understanding allows for adjustments in variable expenses in response to revenue changes, keeping your budget adaptable.

Implement Rolling Forecasts. Instead of static annual budgets, use rolling forecasts that update regularly (e.g., weekly, monthly, or quarterly). This approach allows for continuous adjustment based on actual performance and changing conditions. Also use zero-based budgeting. Start each budgeting period with a "zero base," where all expenses must be justified for each new period, rather than simply adjusting past budgets. *This encourages scrutinizing all expenses and reallocating funds more flexibly.*

PERSEVERANCE PRESSURE

If you don't abide by your budget and spend more than you projected, even with improved volume, there's a common name for this: bankruptcy.

Takeaway

By implementing these strategies, you can create a budgeting process that is not only responsive to the current financial environment, but also robust enough to support decision-making and strategic planning in uncertain times. Profit, nonprofit, academic, large, small: Every organization has to stay within its budget in order to thrive.

Regular Financial Checks

Conduct weekly or monthly cash flow analyses to monitor the inflow and outflow of cash. Understanding your cash flow patterns helps identify potential shortfalls and allows for timely adjustments.

Budget Review: Compare actual revenues and expenses against your budget regularly. This helps in identifying variances early and adjusting your budget or strategy accordingly.

With that comes expense auditing to regularly review your expenses and identify areas of overspending or potential cost savings. Even small reductions in expenses can significantly impact your bottom line.

Review your debt levels and repayment schedules frequently. Assess the cost of debt and explore options for refinancing or consolidation to reduce interest payments or extend repayment terms. As we noted before, inventory should involve regular checks to ensure that inventory levels are aligned with current demand forecasts. Overstocking ties up cash and increases interest payments on loans, while understocking can lead to lost sales.

Monitor accounts receivable closely to ensure that payments are being collected in a timely manner. Implement strategies to reduce the days sales outstanding (DSO) to improve cash flow. Also, adjust your billing so that you're paid promptly and early. The best position is to be paid in advance; the worst is to be paid after completion.

PERSEVERANCE PRESSURE

If your clients or customers are having financial problems, don't give too much leeway, because you'll then go to the bottom of their priorities for payments!

Review accounts payable to manage your outgoing payments effectively. Prioritize payments to take advantage of early payment discounts or to avoid late fees.

Keep abreast of tax obligations and deadlines. Regular checks can help you plan for tax payments and avoid penalties for late submission or underpayment of taxes. Calculate and monitor key financial ratios such as the current ratio, debt-to-equity ratio, and gross profit margin. These ratios provide insights into the financial health and performance of your business.

Forecasting: Update your financial forecasts regularly based on the latest available data. Accurate forecasting helps in anticipating future financial needs and challenges, allowing for proactive management.

Takeaway

Incorporating these regular financial checks into your business practices can provide you with a clearer understanding of your financial position. This clarity will enable you to make informed decisions and navigate through challenging times more effectively.

Scenario Planning for Uncertainties

Start by identifying the key variables that could impact your financial situation, such as market demand, cost of goods, or regulatory changes. Understanding these variables helps in constructing realistic scenarios. Create multiple scenarios based on possible future states of each key variable. Typically, scenarios include a best-case, worst-case, and most likely case to cover a range of possibilities.

For each scenario, quantify the potential financial impact on your business. This includes changes in revenue, expenses, cash flow, and profitability. Then assign a probability to each scenario based on how likely you believe it is to occur. This helps in prioritizing planning efforts towards the most probable outcomes. Also consider the degree of seriousness (or opportunity) that it may present.

Develop contingency plans for each scenario. These plans should outline specific actions to take if the scenario begins to unfold, helping to mitigate risks or capitalize on opportunities.

Scenario planning needn't be overly detailed, but it is vital in these tumultuous times. Demographics, social mores, the economy, technology, natural disasters, and other factors are no longer uncommon occurrences.

PERSEVERANCE PRESSURE

Never assume that you've covered all the bases with your normal planning.

Identify and monitor trigger points that would indicate a particular scenario is becoming more likely. This could include economic indicators, competitive actions, or internal performance metrics. It's wise to follow experts in finance, geopolitics, supply chain, talent acquisition, and so forth to help you—but only those who have a sterling track record. Think Warren Buffet.

Conduct stress tests on your financial models to understand how different scenarios would affect your liquidity, solvency, and overall financial health. Now develop a communication plan for each scenario, detailing how you will communicate with stakeholders (employees, investors, customers, suppliers, bankers, relatives in family businesses) about changes in the business environment and your response strategies.

Takeaway

Scenario planning is an insurance policy that helps in the event you haven't considered all the variables—or given them sufficient weight—in your normal planning activities.

Including these points in your planning will provide you and your key people with a comprehensive guide to using scenario planning as a strategic tool for managing financial uncertainty and making informed decisions during challenging times.

Seek Professional Advice

Professional advisors offer an objective perspective on your financial situation, helping to identify issues and opportunities you might overlook. (Note that these are not "advisory council" or "board" people, but people you pay to provide objective expertise.)

Financial professionals bring expertise in specialized areas such as tax planning, legal structures, and investment strategies, which are crucial for informed decision-making. Advisors can help identify potential financial risks and provide strategies to mitigate them, protecting your business from unforeseen challenges. Professionals can advise on tax-efficient structures and strategies, ensuring you're not only compliant but also maximizing your tax benefits.

PERSEVERANCE PRESSURE

If you're in the graphics design business, you wouldn't expect a client to do their own graphics design as well as you could, or in the floor installation business to expect do-it-yourself floor installers to do a better job. Why would you try to do your own taxes, for example?

Expert advice on managing cash flow can be invaluable, especially in times of financial uncertainty, helping to ensure that your business remains solvent. If your business is facing high levels of debt, business advisors can offer solutions for restructuring that debt to more manageable levels.

Professionals often have networks and resources that can be beneficial for your business, including access to funding sources or strategic partners. Staying compliant with ever-changing regulations can be complex. Professional advisors ensure that your business meets all legal and financial requirements.

For businesses looking to transition ownership or leadership, business advisors can guide the planning process to ensure a smooth and financially sound changeover. Establishing a relationship with a business advisor means you have ongoing access to advice and support as your business and the external environment evolve.

Takeaway

Professional financial advice plays a critical role in navigating challenging times. It helps business owners to make informed decisions, manage risks, and position their businesses for resilience and growth.

Note

1 Prior to age 70, you're much more likely to suffer disability than death. Good news/bad news!

Chapter 4

Diversifying Revenue Streams

Identify New Opportunities

Leverage direct feedback from your current customer base to uncover new problems they need solving. This can lead to the development of new products or services. Remember that your clients and customers always seem to know what they *want,* but don't always know what they *need.* For example, you might want to replace a salesperson who left unexpectedly. But the real need may be in determining how they will be selling in the *future,* and whether increasing online sales might dictate hiring a technologist and declining personal sales might justify a smaller sales force.

Figure 4.1 shows your *value distance,*[1] as an executive or even an employee, when raising such questions and justifying your own leadership ability and worth.

Use the same approach with your own customers, who may simply be going through the process of reordering what is actually not as important as what they should be ordering for a different future. Do you really need more office furniture if your employees are increasingly remote, or another rental car contract if Uber is cheaper?

PERSEVERANCE PRESSURE

Things can change quickly and what you "want" is no longer as important. Pharmaceutical sales forces once sold to hospital executives

DOI: 10.4324/9781003616597-5

and doctors in medical practices, often offering lucrative free samples and trips to "conferences" in vacation resorts. Today, sales are made in the "basement" to procurement people paid to pressure for the lowest price.

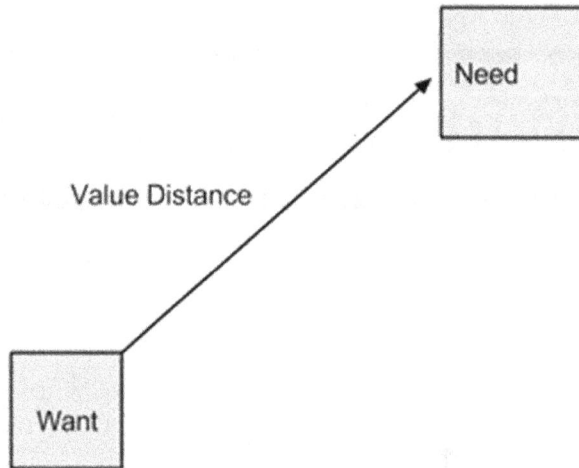

Figure 4.1 Value distance.

Analyze your competitors to identify gaps in their offerings or areas where your business can provide a superior solution. This analysis can provide a new revenue stream for your business. But be careful about reacting to them. You can't allow competitors to dictate your action in the marketplace.

Avis proudly promoted that it was "Number Two" (after Hertz). But Enterprise is now the largest rental car business in the country because, building on its origins of providing cars for insurance claims temporary substitutes, it began delivering cars to rental customers, avoiding the airport lines.

Note that competitors often group together in the same neighborhoods: fast food chains, car dealerships, even dive bars. Visit the competition, *but don't try to do something better than they're already doing. Try to do something new and different that only you can do.* Examples:

- Dry cleaners who deal with commuters from a van at train stations.
- Same-day delivery from local hardware stores.
- Pick-up and delivery of cars at homes for servicing.
- Lounges that offer free olives, chips, and nuts with your drinks at the bar.

Analyze your competitors to stand out from them in a crowd, not to be like them and just be one of the crowd.

Conduct thorough market research to identify emerging trends, underserved niches, and customer needs that are not currently being met by your existing products or services. Here are some inexpensive ways to do that:

■ **Shop your competitors' businesses.** (If you might be recognized, send in someone else.) There are even professional "competitive shoppers" if you want to invest. See how customers are met and supported. Ask to see samples. Find out about payment terms. Call the customer service numbers. Contact them on the internet. If it's an inexpensive product or service, place an order. Then compare your similar actions to the competition. Are you worse? The same? Better? Better is the only desired outcome!

■ **Check out your competitors' advertising and promotions.** What do they offer? Do they stress price, or quality, or timing, or something else? (Don't forget *you really might need an item or service, so you might become an actual customer!*)

■ **Hire a consulting firm.** They can survey your present and past customers, as well as non-customers to find out what they feel about you and about your direct competition. You've probably already received such surveys from certain airlines, hotels, and credit card companies which ask if the recipient would compare their business to competitive businesses. (Some will go so far as to assemble in-person or remote focus groups, which they will tape and record.)

VIGNETTE

Some years ago, an advertising firm in New York commissioned a firm to judge their clients' perception of their quality and also to measure the firms' expectations of what clients would say. *It turned out that the clients had a higher rating of the ad firm's quality than the firm itself did.* That meant that the firm was probably undercharging and over-delivering. That's an example of market research on your own business that can immediately improve profitability.

Stay abreast of technological advancements in your sector. These can open up new avenues for product development, service delivery, and customer engagement. You may need help for this. For example, AI is seen by some as an answer to all prayers, and by others as a warning that the sky is falling. You'll need an expert to suggest where and what technology can improve your business, and also what and where to stay away from.

For example, business contracts, proposals, instruction sheets, warranties, and product updates can be reliably conveyed using ChatGPT or a related technology. But targeted promotional pieces, discount offerings to top customers, responses to complaints, and holiday greetings are best done with human design. (The technology here helps with the dissemination, not the creation.)

Moreover technology "morphs" almost daily, and it can be as dangerous and unprofitable to over-employ as it is to underutilize. It will probably be more and more important, however, to find people for the business who are technologically adept.

Isn't it astounding how many airline gate agents can only type with two fingers, when using a keyboard is probably the most essential part of their jobs? Would you hire a bus driver without a driver's license or a bartender who doesn't know how to mix drinks?

Monitor Changes in Regulations Within Your Industry. These can create opportunities for new services or products that help customers navigate these changes. The changes can be municipal, county, state, regional, or federal. When President Trump was elected in 2024 there were myriad actions being considered by all kinds of organizations in anticipation of *what he might do* even though he didn't take office until mid-January 2025.

It's a good idea to have solid relationships with local politicians in order to learn the real "scoop" about what's likely. This doesn't have to be 100 percent accurate, so long as it rules out the extremes and provides a reasonable range of actions for you to consider.

Takeaways

Identifying new opportunities for revenue diversification requires a proactive approach. Focus on innovation, customer needs, and market dynamics. By continuously exploring these areas, businesses can uncover valuable opportunities to expand their revenue streams. They will reduce dependency on a single source of income and build a more resilient business model.

Mitigate Financial Risks

Reduce your dependence on "single sources." By not relying on a single product, service, or customer for the majority of revenue, a business can protect itself from significant financial impact if that source diminishes or is usurped.

A single supplier can go out of business. The *Providence Journal,* a Pulitzer Prize-winning daily newspaper in Providence, RI had to close a printing operation and let over a hundred people go when their sole supplier of a certain kind of printing plate ended production. The newspaper was its only customer for that obsolescing printing plate and it was no longer profitable for the supplier to produce.

Walk-in clinics have become popular, but their growth may well be curtailed as telehealth flourishes, especially with huge competition from the likes of Amazon and other retailers. Many small businesses lost their sole sources of credit when banks failed or were taken over during financial crises over the last two decades.

The strategy to mitigate risks such as these would include producing new products and services, as well as diversifying customers. The Boy Scouts have invited young women into their organization (despite the existence of the Girl Scouts) under "Scouting America."

Before the advent of Airbus, airlines around the world had to depend on one major airframe manufacturer: Boeing. That meant that if Boeing was delayed in delivering planes those airlines' plans and profits might quickly be radically altered. (And even with two such manufacturers today, it's still often a huge risk).

Similar to investment diversification, having multiple revenue streams spreads financial risk. If one stream underperforms, other streams can compensate. Revenue streams can include:

■ **Adding related services.** Uber carries passengers, delivers food, provides for weddings and special events, drives trucks, and so forth. How long before, in a society of reduced labor resources to possess in-house, they provide airplane captains or ferry captains, or even EMT drivers?

- **Adding related products.** Even hospitals have revenue streams from "merch" (merchandise becoming so important that it has its own shorthand), such as gifts, games, good, batteries, and so forth.
- **Enlarging the activity.** Minor league baseball teams have installed hot tubs, open-air restaurants, and meeting spaces, and major league teams make a great deal selling "skyboxes" and private suites.
- **Creating multiple uses of venues.** Multiplex movie theaters often use empty spaces for comedy clubs, business meetings, amateur productions, and parties.
- **Utilizing waiting times.** Auto dealerships have installed manicurists, barbers, and masseuses in refurbished waiting areas in their service departments.

This kind of diversification can open up avenues for growth and scaling that wouldn't be possible if a business were confined to a single niche or market. The most glaring example of this on a large scale is Amazon, originally a bookseller who branched out into a myriad of retail merchandise and services, most recently breaking into the telehealth arena.

Watching trends and others' success doesn't necessitate trying to do what they're doing in a better way (which is often impossible, since they were the originators). However, consider these strong growth areas *and the attendant success in related services and products:*

- **Smart phones:** Apps, cases, warranties, screen repair, designer cases
- **Pickleball:** Equipment, clothing, lessons, injury treatments
- **Tourism:** Clothing, personal guides, audible tours, all-inclusive resorts
- **IRAs and investments:** Counseling, estate planning, tax attorneys
- **Beauty:** Hair, manicures, facials, Pilates, massage, accessories
- **Exercise:** Clothing, personal trainers, clubs, safety, equipment

These are examples of diversifying your business based on trends and pursuits that don't originate with you, or even with your own industry or market. They are *complementary* to the successes that others are already enjoying.

Multiple revenue streams can lead to more consistent cash flow in that seasonal or cyclical downturns in one area can be offset by gains in another. Some revenue streams may be independent while some may be complementary. And while some may seem to be tangential, they can be major earners for you.

For example, stores such as Best Buy and mega-operations such as Apple, as well as small retailers like jewelers, offer warranties and guarantees. They are often perceived as inexpensive—say, $149 for a three-year warranty on a $2,000 large-screen, "smart" TV—yet two issues are important:

1. *This is additional revenue at point of sale.* Even perceived small amounts add up to huge revenue sources over the course of a year.
2. *They are seldom used, so there is almost pure margin involved.* This is like the postal service selling stamps designed to appeal to philatelists so that there is no postal service or labor ever involved with them, and the sole expense is the printing, which costs a fraction of a penny per stamp.

We've mentioned above the power of "merch" to enhance revenue, which we can see in every bar, gym, and ballpark selling everything from hats to shirts, from coffee mugs to clothing. Many associations, such as for car enthusiasts, make a huge amount of money from such "merch."

If you notice that your paper bills from all kinds of credit operations and stores also contain advertising and offers from completely different businesses, it's because *the circulation and distribution of the bills are also a means of selling advertising space to non-competitive organizations!*

Hence, be as creative as possible with diverse revenue possibilities!

Finally, operating in various markets or sectors can provide valuable data and insights. It can help businesses make informed strategic decisions and further mitigate risks.

The old days of taking a month to set a strategy that reached into the next five or ten years are long gone. Agility and resilience are the keys today. Thus, you have to be constantly in touch with *real-world* events and changes to be able to adjust—and even anticipate and prepare in many cases. That won't come from the internet, or even the daily news outlets.

It will come instead from your monitoring the habits and performance of your customers, particularly their frequency of ordering, trends, suggestions, referrals, and returns (complaints). You'll be able to pick up trends and changes in direction not only more rapidly, *but as they specifically relate to your business and your strategy over the coming year.*

Diagnose what your customers are inadvertently revealing, no less than a doctor checks heartbeat, pulse, and other vitals. The failure to do so can allow your enterprise to become ill. The discipline to do so can ensure a long and healthy life.

Takeaways

Putting in place a strategy to diversify revenue streams can significantly contribute to a business's financial health and operational resilience.

Increase Market Competitiveness

We should all attempt to optimize resource diversification. By diversifying, businesses can more efficiently use their resources (e.g., technology, personnel). This will increase productivity and competitive advantage.

Traditionally, organizations viewed people as expenses and equipment as assets. Hence, "preventive maintenance" was performed on machines, not people. We know today that people are the assets. Consequently, diversifying efforts would include initiatives such as cross-training, so that one person can fulfill another's job. While we wouldn't expect flight attendants to perform as pilots (or vice versa!), why wouldn't we expect field engineers helping with continuous flow processes to also recommend other products and services from their company? After all, who is more familiar with their actual implementation and usage?

Banks have sometimes introduced the "360° banker," meaning one person, one contact, for *all* of a customer's needs. That banker may not know investing as well as mortgage work, or lines of credit as well as online technology, but they do have quick access to people who do, thereby preventing the customer from having to deal with many different people (and phone queues).

Optimization of resources also pertains to raw materials or time. You may find suppliers who can provide a multitude of products and services for you at discounted rates, rather than doing business with six different vendors. Have you ever gone on "errands" that involve both your company and your personal needs? This is the same principle.

The more you take control of your marketing, the less vulnerable you are to market cycles. Some of these are normal and inexorable, such as seasons, "influencers" and normative pressures, and special events and holidays. Others are almost mythological, such as, "No one is around during the holidays" or "This item will have consistent appeal."

Multiple revenue streams can mitigate the impact of market or seasonal cycles. This can ensure steady performance against competitors who may be more affected by such fluctuations. In the retail business, it seems crazy to simply surrender to the maxim that 75 percent of annual revenue is in the fourth quarter and 75 percent of that is in December!

Similarly, realtors have found that the traditional, sacrosanct six percent commission is now in the trash, and they now must compete on value for smaller percentages.

Diversification can open opportunities for strategic partnerships with other businesses to expand reach and enhance competitive positioning. Some people refer to "channel marketing" and some to "alliances." We've already mentioned that businesses selling smart phones will probably agree to sell smart phone cases, ear buds, and other such accessories.

The masters of diversification would be the "Big Box" retailers like BJ's or Costco, where you can wander the aisles and purchase tires, eyeglasses, fresh food, best-selling books, deodorant, clothing, and so forth. (Amazon, of course, is the master of this online.) Every gas station, it seems, now houses a "mini-mart," which is often visited even if customers don't need gas. It's hard to find a beauty shop that isn't only offering facials and massages, but also products for your entire body! Bookstores (and jewelers) are offering coffee and pastry.

There's a big difference between "customer-focus" and "market-focus." The former is about adding products and services attractive to your current and prospective customers. A laundry might also include dry cleaning, or home delivery, or discounted cleaning products. A jeweler might include appraisals, repairs, and cleaning.

The latter, however, involves a market beyond just a customer. For example, Gillette is in the men's toiletry market, going far beyond blades to include deodorant, lotions, beard care, and so forth. They've made forays into the greater grooming market by adding women's products, such as facial hair removal, skin products, and bikini razors. (Once upon a time, Playboy Enterprises sold subscriptions, clothing, club memberships, and magazines to its men's marketplace.)

We are talking about diverse and agile market response and innovation. Diverse revenue sources provide the flexibility to quickly adapt to market changes. This allows businesses to seize new opportunities or mitigate risks faster than competitors. Instead of merely reacting to changing market conditions, you can affect market conditions to your advantage. That's why each new "smart phone" offers still more value with more unique features.

The belief that your customer is "fixed" and will not change defies demographic, cultural, and technological realities!

Takeaways
Implementing a diversification strategy secures the current market position of a business and helps pave the way for future growth and competitiveness.

Leverage Existing Resources

Conduct a thorough assessment of your existing resources, including intellectual property, customer base, and physical assets, to identify underutilized areas with potential for revenue generation. Especially if you've been in business for two years or more, you probably have extensive customer information, supplier information, and marketing experiences which may be useful. (Example: Past prospective vendors who may be more economical than your existing ones today.)

Identify unique skills or knowledge within your team that can be transformed into new products or services, such as specialized training or consulting. Especially in the services area, can some of your employees provide a win/win/win situation for themselves, the customers, and you? What if one of your hair stylists can also provide clothing advice, or a trainer is licensed in certain testing instruments?

If you have physical assets, consider how they can be used differently or rented out to generate additional income. This could include office space, equipment, or other materials. Movie theaters rent out empty auditoriums, snowplows can be leased to the local government, accounting firms can rent empty offices to clients who don't have their own.

Collaborate with business partners or affiliates to cross-promote products or services. Leverage each other's customer bases and resources for mutual benefit. Examples would be a law firm offering a free Zoom session on investing from an accounting firm, or a real estate firm providing access to a design firm.

Leverage feedback from your current customer base to identify new needs or problems you can solve, leading to the development of new offerings. Your customers and clients comprise your "laboratory" so that you can try new products and services, solicit design help, and run pilot programs. This can be especially useful when considering discounts, bonus offerings, and so forth.

Takeaways

By thoughtfully leveraging your existing resources, you can uncover new opportunities for revenue diversification without the need for significant additional investment, which can pave the way for sustainable growth.

Note

1 *Value Based Fees*, Alan Weiss, John Wiley, 2021.

Chapter 5

Embracing Digital Transformation and Streamlining Operations for Efficiency

The Importance of Digital Transformation for Small Business

Digital tools automate routine tasks, which can free up valuable time for strategic work and thus increase overall operational efficiency. In both the product and services realms, digital technology can add to (and sometimes revolutionize):

- Inventory control
- Customer communications
- Government compliance
- Fiscal management
- Safety and security
- Theft reduction
- Delivery and tracking
- Returns and refunds
- Pricing adjustments (think of "surge pricing")

DOI: 10.4324/9781003616597-6

- Real-time progress and performance metrics
- Online and remote sales, service, and customer inquiry

Hence, the "high tech/high touch" dynamic leans toward high tech here.

Let's focus for the moment on the customer. Digital platforms enable personalized and seamless customer interactions across multiple channels, which improve satisfaction and loyalty. You have, no doubt, used such mechanisms yourself for ordering products and services. In many cases, same-day or next-day deliveries are made (Staples and Amazon, for example, are famous for this).

We return to the "high tech/high touch" dynamic by pointing out that robotized chats and responses are offered (which are adequate, but not outstanding), as well as "live" chats with agents which can be outstanding. (A T-Mobile issue forced me to call their service line. I put the response on speaker and opened my internet browser. Before I could read a single article, an agent was on the phone assuring me she could fix the problem, and she did so in the next three minutes.)

PERSEVERANCE PRESSURE

The idea of digital customer service is to enable solutions, sales, and feedback without direct human intervention, and to provide that intervention access when it is clearly required for optimal customer service. *This is a light dimmer, not an "on/off" switch.*

Data-driven decision-making means leveraging digital analytics tools to provide insights into customer behavior, market trends, and operational performance. This allows for more informed and strategic decision-making. At the moment, it's most famous (or infamous) in sports, where football coaches know when it's best to "go for it" on fourth down, and baseball coaches take pitchers out after a designated number of pitches (even, in some cases, if they're pitching a no-hitter).

If you extrapolate this, one wonders why the coach is necessary at all. But there is some wisdom in the usage of data in decisions. They can give you a norm for customer behavior so that you can discern if there is a positive or negative departure and find the cause—eliminating problems and exploiting opportunities. There are huge benefits in reducing inventory costs, whether hardware, clothing, or automobiles.

Standardized testing has long been applied to job applicants for promotion candidates. Data itself is neither good nor bad, it's how that data is used that represents help or harm. Receiving a digital report on your car's oil life, tire inflation, and warranty status is far better than having to check manually each month. But when you're unsure about something, calling the service manager is usually the best route.

Digital transformation makes your business accessible to a global audience. It breaks down geographical barriers and opens up new markets. There have never been opportunities like this before. Even during the pandemic, many businesses thrived through remote purchasing and delivery.

To enable this still further, digital solutions include purchasing online that automatically fills in billing and shipping information. Products are often delivered the next day, services sometimes the same day. (And using a fingerprint, as is the case with most Apple devices, makes this easier and safer than ever.)

"Digital Black Friday" rivals traditional "Black Friday" in holiday spending.

All of this creates huge cost reductions. By streamlining operations and reducing manual tasks, digital technologies can significantly lower operational costs over time, including:

- Fewer employees required for the job
- Fewer skilled employees required for many jobs (technician vs. salesperson)
- Fewer expensive employees required for many jobs with more front-line people but fewer managers and executives. (The latest cutbacks at FedEx® and UPS® were in "white collar" ranks, not "blue collar" or union ranks.)
- Customers who can help themselves on digital platforms
- More efficient inventory control and "just-in-time" stocking
- Tracking of more profitable products and services
- Information for pricing strategies

As you can see, cost reductions can add as much to margins as increased revenues with far less investment (digital assistance stays in place; humans are required for increasing revenues in many cases).

Digital tools allow businesses to be more agile, adapting quickly to market changes or customer needs with minimal disruption. Some issues are predictable and you can prepare for them: seasonal shifts, technology evolutions (as opposed to "breakthroughs"), consumer spending (based on inflation, unemployment, and so forth). But some issues emerge surprisingly and with great influence.

We have a new emphasis on legal gambling, actually advertised on television and accessible in smart phones and tablets *during games.* There is the Taylor Swift phenomenon. People have traveled to Warsaw and Paris with their kids because it's cheaper to do that than try to buy tickets to her concerts in the US. Telehealth, talked about for some time, suddenly accelerated with the entry of Amazon into the market.

Digital platforms facilitate better communication and collaboration within teams—regardless of their physical location—leading to increased productivity and innovation. The new remote and hybrid work environments require much more proactivity among employees—there is no more gathering around the coffee machine or talking over cubicle walls. But common internal technologies can remedy a great deal of that. "Intranets" serve within organizations, large and small, to enable employees to talk to each other and also to "talk" to processes (inventory, margins, buying trends) easily.

Digital solutions can easily scale with your business growth, supporting more customers, products, or services without a proportional increase in costs or complexity. Scalability—the ability to exponentially increase contacts, sales, and information access—is vital for all businesses, but especially essential for smaller businesses. There are economies of scale possible that couldn't be achieved earlier.

The food delivery that you receive not directly from the restaurant but via a third-party specializing in the actual delivery service is a simple example of scaling a restaurant's dinner business.

Finally, we'll mention regulatory changes. You'll want to monitor changes in regulations within your industry. They can create opportunities for new services or products that help customers navigate these changes. This applies to travel agents with TSA and visa concerns or airline schedule shifts, or to shippers who make decisions based on rail or truck options. Regulation monitoring is also vital for financial planning in terms of taxes, foreign exchange rates, and so forth.

Takeaways

Incorporating digital transformation into your business strategy is not just about adopting new technologies; it's about reshaping your operations, culture, and customer interactions to thrive in the digital age.

Assessment and Identification of Inefficiencies in Current Operations

Examine your current workflows to pinpoint bottlenecks, redundant tasks, or processes that consume excessive time and resources without adding value. (Don't forget that a "large bottleneck" is an oxymoron!) We often fall into inefficient work protocols and processes because, "We've always done it this way."

Here's a good test: Does everyone "touching" a communication, or provision of a service, or product development and sale *add value to it?* Many people are at meetings they needn't attend (just because their name is on the invitation), or they have to approve something that doesn't require their expertise, or involve themselves with things their subordinates should be handling.

A frequent example is not providing enough empowerment to front-line people so that a reasonable customer request or even complaint must "go up the chain of command." This takes the time of people who will almost always agree with a subordinate's decision on how to handle the issue, or they'll suggest a resolution that a lower-level person could have provided if they had been given the authority to do so.

One easy way to examine and improve workflow is to try to "manage by exception," meaning that you step in only when absolutely needed to resolve an issue. The opposite of this—routinely stepping in—is known by another term: micromanagement.

Assess how effectively your business is using existing technology. Look for outdated systems that slow down operations or areas where manual processes could be automated. I visit a coffee shop where the proprietor keeps hitting his electronic register as if he's in a battle with the keyboard. After several failed attempts to come up with a price and tax, he always says, "Just give me four dollars."

That's quaint on Main Street, but what if that is happening with your inventory or sales records, or promotional campaigns? Have you "cleansed" your mailing lists, or verified your profit reports, or compared your actual budgeted expenses against actual expense reporting?

Technology (and its upgrades) for its own sake is often a waste of time and money. You've seen the editing software on your computer, no doubt, but it isn't something you'd ever use for your photos or movies. You can record a rock concert, but you just need to record business meetings. *And we all have features on our cars we never use, can't find, or don't know that they're there.*

Start with the question, "What do I need, and how often?" and then ask, "What are the best options and sources?" (e.g., customers, employees, competition, marketplace, and so forth). Finally, ask, "What is the best option to gather, analyze, and use this for business improvement?"

Business software, in particular, is an expensive proposition and usually causes disruption as it's upgraded or changed. Assess your effectiveness and the time span needed to see potential improvements, and then make your decisions. Don't bow to "the latest" or "suggested upgrades." Find out what's right for you. If you don't have a technical person on staff, engage an outside consultant *who doesn't sell any hardware or software, but solely makes recommendations based on efficiencies.*

Engage with your team to collect insights into challenges they face in their day-to-day tasks. Often, those working directly with processes can highlight inefficiencies not immediately apparent to management.

Your most important people are "front-line" people who interface with the customer or client regularly—in person, by phone, on the internet, by live chats, by Zoom. Ask them these questions:

■ "What tools or skills do you need that you don't have now that would most help you with a customer's questions, complaints, or orders?"
■ "What is the most common kind of feedback you receive from customers?"
■ "Would you be comfortable providing product and service knowledge to customers and suggesting they purchase such value?"
■ "In what mode (phone, Zoom, chat, etc.) do you feel you are most successful in helping the customer and the customer is the most satisfied with the interaction?"
■ "Can you resolve most issues (90+%) during your interactions? Or, do more than 10% of issues have to be passed on to superiors?"
■ "Do you commonly know our customers by their names? Are they recognizable?"

Analyze customer feedback and interactions to identify any pain points or delays in service delivery that could indicate operational inefficiencies. Call this a "customer experience evaluation."

You can't always be sure that the value that a customer perceives is the same value you perceive. A cargo cover in my car isn't of value to me because my windows are tinted, but cameras and proximity indicators are of great value. Some people may love ordering take-out food in advance, but some may prefer to have it delivered.

Surveys or interviews or focus groups of customers shouldn't be quantitatively measured. That is, on a scale of one-to-ten, my four may be your seven. You have to provide a common metric: "A four means that you seldom experience this, and a seven means you usually experience it." (And a one means never, and a ten means always. You get the idea.)

You'll also need qualitative feedback to encourage specific comments:

- "Your cashier in the afternoons doesn't seem to know where various items are in the store."
- "The woman answering the phone at 4:50pm on Wednesday told me to hurry up; she plans to leave at 5pm."

Along with asking your customers comes shopping your business. You can do this with external help, or with managers who might not be recognized. Call the company main number, make a complaint about a product, see how long you're offered help after you walk in the store, try to return something, and ask other, "real" customers why they shop there.

Remember the show, *Undercover Boss*? That's what we're talking about!

For the best data management practices, review how data is collected, stored, and accessed within your organization. Inefficient data management can lead to duplicated efforts and difficulty in making informed decisions. Who is accountable for collecting what information? Always remember that effective data management depends on *why* the data is needed and for what purposes it is to be utilized.

Assess your supply chain and vendor relationships to identify any delays, quality issues, or costs that could be optimized for better efficiency. Review this data every quarter against the metrics and standards you've established to ensure timeliness and quality for your business. If you don't have such metrics, create them and share them with your vendors. Low cost shouldn't be the main selection criterion.

Takeaway

By thoroughly assessing these areas, you can identify key inefficiencies within your operations and prioritize them for improvement through digital transformation and streamlined processes. This proactive approach not only enhances operational efficiency, but also positions your business for sustainable growth and competitiveness.

Process Optimization and Automation

Begin such optimization by identifying repetitive, time-consuming tasks within your operations that have potential for automation, such as data entry, invoicing, or customer notifications.

Ask yourself how long they've been in place without upgrade or change, or, for that matter, how long since you've asked that question. You're likely to find eligible components for improvement. Visually map out existing processes to understand the flow of tasks, information, and decisions. This helps in identifying inefficiencies and areas where automation can streamline operations. Ask others' opinions about the work flow. *What you believe to be the case may not actually be true in daily reality.* Someone once told us, "You don't have on your process map that the distribution manager has to approve these shipments, which usually takes at least an extra day."

Define specific, measurable goals for your process optimization and automation efforts. These goals can include reducing process time by a certain percentage, improving accuracy, or enhancing customer satisfaction. Choose the correct tools for improvement. Research and select technology solutions that align with your business needs and objectives. Consider scalability, integration capabilities, and user-friendliness in your selection criteria. Don't default to technology—sometimes taking people out of the flow can make huge improvements without any detriment. Ask: Why is this person "touching" (involved in) this flow or process? Do they add any value?

Engage employees, customers, and other stakeholders in the automation process to gather insights, ensure buy-in, and minimize resistance to change. You can easily also involve customers—who love to tell you why something takes too long, is inaccurate, or doesn't perform well. If you use customer surveys routinely, add questions related to these issues and potential improvements. Remember that if you change a process in error, you can usually change it back!

PERSEVERANCE PRESSURE

Even the best processes can deteriorate or become obsolete. Just consider how people pay for things today, in the store or remotely, as compared to a few years ago.

In automating processes, prioritize solutions that enhance the user experience for both employees and customers, making interactions smoother and more efficient. Roll out automation in phases, starting with less complex processes to gain momentum, and allow for learning and adjustments before tackling more significant changes.

Keep everyone closely apprised of what you're doing. Years ago, Cadillac announced a tricky, new convertible and high-potential buyers were invited for test drives. However, when many showed up at the dealerships, the service team hadn't been trained in how to raise or lower the top and had to learn in front of bored potential customers!

Establish metrics to monitor the impact of process optimization and automation. These metrics can include process completion times, error rates, and customer satisfaction. Confirm that objectives are being met. Treat process optimization and automation as ongoing efforts. Regularly review and refine automated processes to adapt to changing business needs and take advantage of new technological advancements. Provide comprehensive training and support for employees to adapt to new tools and processes. Ensuring they are comfortable and proficient with the changes is key to maximizing the benefits of automation.

Takeaway

By focusing on these areas, businesses can effectively leverage process optimization and automation to streamline operations, reduce costs, and improve overall efficiency and competitiveness in the digital age.

Employee Engagement and Training

Prioritize the focus by keeping employees informed about digital transformation initiatives, the reasons behind them, and the expected outcomes. Transparent communication fosters a culture of trust and inclusion. Develop training programs tailored to the specific needs of different roles within the organization. Customization increases relevance and effectiveness, enhancing employee engagement. A huge advantage today is that you can utilize interactive learning tools and platforms *to make training engaging and practical.* Interactive sessions help in retaining information and applying it in real-world scenarios.

Encourage a culture of continuous learning and improvement. Support employees in pursuing relevant certifications, attending workshops, and staying updated with industry trends. Then, implement feedback mechanisms to gather insights from employees on training programs and digital transformation initiatives. Use this feedback to make necessary adjustments and improvements. Acknowledge and reward employees who actively participate in training programs and contribute to digital transformation efforts. Recognition motivates others to engage and contribute. You can make it a requirement for advancement or certain job assignments.

Involve leaders in training sessions, both as participants and as instructors. Leadership involvement demonstrates commitment to the transformation and can inspire employees. Senior people need to serve as avatars and exemplify the need to learn the technology. Identify and address any resistance to change among employees early on. Provide additional support and information to alleviate concerns and highlight the benefits of the transformation. Provide flexible learning options, such as online courses, in-person workshops, and on-demand resources. These options will serve to accommodate different learning preferences and schedules.

Finally, establish metrics to evaluate the effectiveness of training programs, such as employee satisfaction, knowledge retention, and the application of skills in daily tasks. Use these metrics to continuously improve training initiatives, which should never "end," but rather stay current with the latest best practices.

Takeaway

By focusing on these aspects, businesses can ensure that their employees are not only prepared for but also engaged in the digital transformation process. This engagement is crucial for fostering an innovative, efficient, and resilient organizational culture.

Overcoming Common Challenges

There is almost always resistance to change. Address resistance by fostering a culture of openness and continuous learning. Engage employees early in the transformation process by highlighting benefits and providing support to adapt to changes.

People accept change most readily when:
■ *It is in their best interest to make the change.*
■ *They understand the "journey" and the requirements.*

Most people "buy in" to a rosier future, but they are leery about the disruption that the process may involve. Share the path with them and make sure they are comfortable.

Identify skill gaps with a thorough assessment, and then close them with targeted training programs, hiring, or partnerships. Emphasize the importance of digital literacy across the organization. Identify attitude gaps through discussions and close them with coaching and support. As a "litmus test" as to which is which: If an employee *can* do the job if faced with consequences and penalties for non-performance, that's an *attitude* problem. If an employee *cannot* do the job even when faced with such consequences, that's a *skills* problem. You train for skills improvement, but you coach for attitude improvement.

Prioritize initiatives that offer the highest return on investment (ROI) and consider phased implementation to manage costs. Encourage a culture of continuous learning and improvement. Support employees in pursuing relevant certifications, attending workshops, and staying updated with industry trends. Recognition devices such as "employee of the month" are often well-received.

Evaluate the feasibility of integrating legacy systems with new technologies. Where integration is not viable, develop a phased plan for system upgrades or replacements. Develop a clear digital transformation strategy that aligns with your organization's goals. This strategy should include specific objectives, timelines, and metrics for success.

Plan for continuity of operations during the digital transformation process. This may involve running parallel systems or having contingency plans in place to minimize disruptions. Address resistance proactively. Identify and address any resistance to change among employees early. Provide additional support and information to alleviate concerns and highlight the benefits of the transformation. Provide flexible learning options, such as online courses, in-person workshops, and on-demand resources. These options will serve to accommodate different learning preferences and schedules. Establish metrics to evaluate the effectiveness of training programs, such as employee satisfaction, knowledge retention, and the application of skills in daily tasks. Use these metrics to continuously improve training initiatives.

Takeaway

By focusing on these aspects, businesses can ensure that their employees are prepared for and engaged in the digital transformation process. This engagement is crucial for fostering an efficient and resilient organizational culture.

Chapter 6

Customer Retention Strategies

The Importance of Customer Retention

Retained customers tend to buy more over time, which can significantly increase profitability. Studies have shown that even a 5% increase in customer retention can lead to an increase in profits by 25% to 95%.[1] The most expensive cost—the biggest "hit" on margins—is acquisition of new business. But expanded business (and referral business) have very little, if any, costs of acquisition.

Acquiring new customers can be expensive. Focusing on retention reduces the constant need and associated costs of acquiring new customers. This can allow for a more efficient allocation of resources. A loyal customer base provides a more predictable and stable revenue stream. This predictability is crucial for financial planning and long-term business sustainability.

Any planning you create around new customer acquisition is always speculative. Most organizations' "hit rates" on forecasting new business are probably less than 50% accurate because we tend to become wildly excited when prospects merely agree to talk to us! However, predicting existing customers' probable buying habits and amounts is far more accurate because:

- You have a trusting relationship with the buyer.
- You know of their past habits.

DOI: 10.4324/9781003616597-7

■ You have an intimate knowledge of their probably needs.

This is true of dry cleaning, auto repair, accounting, home repairs, and myriad other services—personal and professional, products and services.

PERSEVERANCE PRESSURE

There are two worse conditions than not having a customer. One is having a "bad" customer. And the other is losing a "good" customer.

There is a wonderful dynamic called "Increased Customer Lifetime Value." Focusing on customer retention boosts the lifetime value of customers because retained customers are more likely to make repeat purchases and increase their spending over time, *as well as refer others to you.*

Entire industries—real estate, auto sales, insurance, to name a few—are based heavily on building this kind of evangelism, with customers eager to do more business with you and also singing your praises to others.[2] Solicited referrals require some time and energy, so there are modest costs of acquisition here. But unsolicited referrals—from your evangelists—are nearly cost-free. These efforts have the salutary and peripheral effect of strengthening your brand. My mentor, Alan Weiss, states that:

A brand is how others think of you when you're not around.

Thus, the need for enhanced branding at all stages of your business. Satisfied, loyal customers are more likely to share positive experiences and recommend your business to others. This positivity will enhance your brand's reputation and attract new customers through word-of-mouth. Interestingly, with most surveys and interviews, only very unhappy or very happy people usually answer in large numbers. The "middle" is rarely represented well. That means that you have to have the very happy hugely outnumber the very unhappy, and also work to sway the great, somewhat apathetic middle.

It's easier to sell additional products or services to existing customers who already trust your brand. This provides for both "cross-selling" and "upselling." Effective retention strategies can generate opportunities for upselling and cross-selling which will further increase revenue *and lower costs.* Customers who are loyal to a brand are often less sensitive to price changes. That is, you're seen as a unique value and not a commodity. With rare exception, people view commodities in products or services as options to be evaluated almost entirely on cost—not return, not value. However, their trust and relationship with your brand can outweigh the allure of cheaper alternatives and provide a buffer against price competition.

We've talked about "evangelism." Another way to view these loyal customers and clients is as "activists." Loyal customers can become brand advocates by actively promoting your products or services to others. This community can amplify your marketing efforts and help attract new customers organically. And, in fact, working with you can become a status symbol in and of itself if people see their respected peers (and superiors) doing business with you:

> *Aren't they the most expensive supplier?*
> *Yes, but they're also, by far, the best.*

Hence, customer retention can be seen as more important than employee retention in some respects. After all, high tech may well replace employees (such as bank tellers), and employees may move and try to take customers with them (which happens often with hair stylists). *The more the allegiance and loyalty are to you and your brand, the more your business can sustain such changes.*

No one needs Gucci to be clothed, Mercedes G-wagons for transportation, or Breitling to tell the time (nor, indeed these days, a watch at all!). But there is an emotional appeal to the brand which creates and retains customers. The brand "kinship" is reward enough to sustain customers—no matter the competition, technology, turmoil, or disruption.

A solid base of loyal customers can provide a buffer for "external shocks," such as economic downturns or competitive surprises. Businesses with strong customer retention strategies are often better positioned to navigate challenging times. One of the obvious reasons we often miss is that loyal customers pay on time and buy repeatedly, which means they hugely aid our cash flow. Thriving through bad times is very dependent on cash flow and reserves.

This invokes "total days to cash" (TDTC)[3] which is a measure of how much your money is really worth. In other words, if you're paid in advance (which is why many businesses offer discounts for advance payment, and some actually require it), you have full use of your money immediately. If you're paid in installments during a project or delivery, you have less value in your cash. If you're paid at the conclusion, or paid late, or not paid at all, you're actually losing money.

Loyal customers don't put you in that position. This is why the *investment* in creating customer loyalty has a huge ROI in terms of a reliable and planned cash flow. You can test your own "reliability rating" of customers by calculating not just how much they've paid you over the year, but *also how quickly.* TDTC is an accurate measure of whether your fees and charges are resulting in the real amounts or are devalued by lateness and follow-ups.

Customer relation strategies are important to every business, whether product or service, large or small.

Takeaways
Implementing effective customer retention strategies is not just about keeping customers—it's about building a sustainable, resilient business that can grow and adapt over time while maintaining a loyal customer base, and gaining "full value" for your fees and prices.

Understanding Customer Needs and Expectations

Insight into customer expectations guides the development of products and services that directly address your market's desires. It can ensure relevance and drive customer retention. This lends itself to rapid and economical new product development in many cases.

Instead of launching and testing products, and suffering long commercialization time, involving good customers *during the process* can ensure not only economic development but also result in early sales to those participating. This has been done with food and beverages, cars, construction equipment, clothing—all sorts of things. Resorts often involve customers during the construction and design phase, and also invite them to early accommodations and experiences.

Have you ever been in a hotel room with lighting insufficient to apply makeup or shave, or sometimes to even read in bed? That's because the designers didn't involve actual users and consumers. The aesthetics were great but not the experience, and people don't return for fine aesthetics and poor experiences!

Understanding and meeting customer expectations is key to customer satisfaction. Satisfied customers are more likely to remain loyal, make repeat purchases, and advocate for your brand. Let's go beyond "customer satisfaction" and call it "customer delight."

You can find the statistics all over. My own investigation reveals that about 70 percent of happy customers will share a positive experience with up to seven other people. But negative experiences are shared with 15 people or more. Often, attempts to compensate for poor experiences lead to worse experiences, such as providing a free meal in a hotel which is as bad as the original meal which prompted the complaint, or sending two poor quality products to compensate someone who received a poor quality product to start with!

However, negative experiences *are* important aspects of creating customer delight, as long as you don't repeat them. Organizations which respond *quickly and effectively to complaints* immediately reverse customer feedback to others. After all, no one goes home and brags to friends and family that, "The room service was right on time," but rather that, "The dinner was late, so they sent a new one for free with a bottle of wine."

People who have difficulties with their cars and are forced to bring them in for service turn out to be delighted when the loaner car *is a better one than their own*. Remember that the customer is not always right and not every customer complaint is legitimate, especially when the customer is returning clothing with perspiration stains under the arms!

Understanding present and future customer needs enables anticipating and addressing customer issues before they become complaints or unhappiness, and demonstrates commitment. It can significantly enhance customer trust and loyalty.

It's not the impossible attempt to prevent all problems that's important in customer retention; it's the *rapid response to fix problems that is even more critical*. That's especially true since the cause of the problem may be a third party (suppliers, delivery, internet, and so forth), but you're nevertheless the one who has to "fix" it or compensate for it.

Understanding evolving customer expectations helps your business stay ahead of market trends. This helps your offerings to remain relevant and desirable over time. It also separates fads—a temporary movement toward something transiently popular (pet rocks, hula hoops, mid-calf dresses)—from true trends that have traction and high potential (Zoom sessions, electric vehicles, telehealth).

Finally, you'll be able to track differences in generational needs and movements through the expectations of your customers by using sampling to determine whether customers' expectations will change due to aging, normative pressures, "influencers," and so on.

Customers whose needs and expectations are met are more likely to engage with your brand. They might participate in loyalty programs and take advantage of upselling or cross-selling opportunities. Ultimately, understanding and meeting customer needs lays the foundation for long-term relationships. These relationships are key to sustained business success, as loyal customers are the cornerstone of a resilient business model.

Takeaways

Incorporating a deep understanding of customer needs and expectations into your retention strategies ensures that your business remains customer-centric. It is a critical factor for success in today's competitive business environment.

Personalization and Customer Experience

Personalization helps to create a deeper emotional connection with customers. When customers feel understood and valued, they are more likely to develop loyalty to a brand. And bear in mind that Alan Weiss states that logic makes people think, but emotions make them act.

The more you "curate" the offers to customers—even if by tiers of highest, medium, and lowest in activity—the more personalized the relationship. We see this on the web all the time: "Mary, you've purchased these products in the past, we thought you'd be interested in these as well." (This is as opposed to what Joan or Jill might be interested in). Amazon is great at this, but you don't need their size or sophistication to personalize effectively, and it's often easier to do it with a smaller business.

After all, you *do* know customers by name and can identify them visually in many instances.

No one wants to be treated as an animal in a herd. (This is why elections are won and lost: Politicians assume that all people in a given group will act alike, and that is simply not true. Many of the "Boomer" generation disagree with each other, but agree with many in the "GenZ" generation. And someone like Taylor Swift seems to have appeal across *all* generations!)

Alan Weiss shared a story that there was a time when Bentley bought all new purchasers a bespoke suit. The tailors would come to the buyers' homes for the measurements. Of course, they stood a good chance of developing a future client, but can you think of a better way to show personalized appreciation?

Tailoring products, services, and communications to meet individual customer needs increases the relevance of your offerings. It makes customers more likely to stay engaged and continue using your services. That's because you can also anticipate needs, and even create needs. This moves you from a commodity to a unique value offering, and from *price* to *return on investment.*

All customers know what they want, but they don't always know what they need. Most of us never knew we needed an automatic garage door opener, or a cell phone with video capabilities, or cameras on our cars. But once we experienced them, they became "musts." (Something is a luxury only until it's used successfully a second time, and then it becomes a necessity!)

In the illustration below, which I've repeated from a prior discussion, I'll reinforce the difference between "want" and "need," which may be called the "value distance[4]."

If the value distance is tiny, then there's no premium, no justification for higher prices or fees. But if it's significant *in the eyes of the buyer* then it justifies higher prices and higher margins.

To relate to our prior discussions, *need* often involves being connected emotionally with a powerful brand that supports one's ego. Consequently,

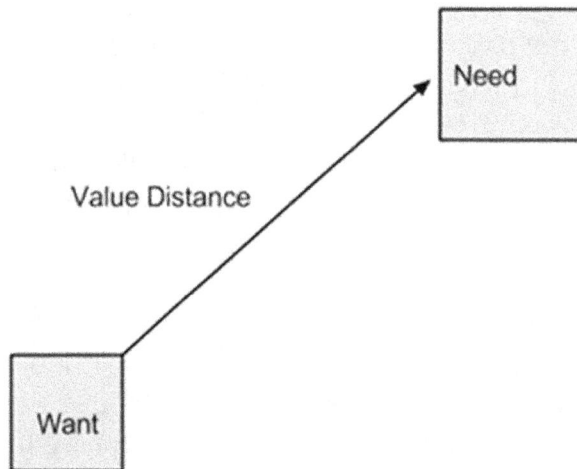

Figure 6.1 The value distance.

customers are often willing to pay more for products and services that are tailored to their specific needs *or fulfill needs of which you have been made aware*. Personalization can thus support a premium pricing strategy which enhances profitability. Consider such needs, which progress from the novel and new to the common and expected:

- Personalized taxi service (Uber)
- Foods of all kind delivered for dinner (Grub Hub)
- Next-day delivery (Amazon)
- Flexible employment (remote work)
- Pet support (removal of dog waste, mobile groomers)
- Remote medical advice (telehealth)
- Real time editing and research (ChatGPT)
- Dietary support (special meals on airplanes)

By making customers feel valued and understood, personalized experiences reduce the likelihood of churn. Companies (and professional associations) that cite "stability" in customers and members often overlook the fact that they've gained ten percent to compensate for a ten percent loss. This obviously is not the route to growth.

Churn occurs very commonly when you don't improve your value, don't add to your offerings of products and services, and don't create new "needs." Your customers ultimately become bored and move on to competitors who either have the same perceived value as you *at lower prices* or who seem to offer *an appeal to an unrecognized need better than you do.*

Churn damages margins because it's so much more expensive to attract and retain a new customer than it is to delight an existing one who reorders. But that requires a philosophy of providing much more than merely meeting *wants*.

Personalized customer support can address individual concerns more effectively and lead to higher satisfaction rates. There are two primary ways to create customer need and to reduce any customer unhappiness:

- **You implement policies and procedures which can help everyone:** User-friendly, intuitive web sites; fast responsiveness to questions and complaints; frequent communications about sales, discounts, and hours of operation; an intelligent returns policy; loyalty programs.

■ **You implement policies and procedures aimed at specific customers and/or situations:** Advance notice of sales for top customers; accessibility in person and online for those who need such help; overdue payment resolutions; specialized and bespoke requests.

No matter how many customers or clients you possess, you can arrange policies in these two areas which should alleviate and prevent complaints and disappointments, and *prevent issues from escalating to require your personal attention.* The more these policies can empower people on the front lines to resolve issues and create new sales, the more you focus on running the business and not being a part of it: focus *on* it, not *in* it.

Personalization can extend to such simple and easy issues as people's initials on consumer goods, special phone lines for help, extended hours on occasion, or even the attention of an assigned sales or service person (the best banks do this very well).

In a crowded market, personalization can help your brand stand out by offering unique, tailored experiences that competitors may not provide. This differentiation is key to attracting and retaining customers.

While it's true that a high level of competition *expands markets and does not narrow them,* nevertheless, you need to "stand out in the crowd." Burger King may be across the road from McDonald's (or one auto repair shop next to another), but they nonetheless try to differentiate themselves. If they attempt to do so solely on price, it's a long descent into razor-thin margins, or high debt, or bankruptcy.

Below you'll find a representation of this from my mentor, Alan Weiss:

As you can see in the example for a professional services firm, as you move from left to right you further distinguish yourself even in a crowded field or market. At the extreme right would be your "vault" which contains unique offerings from you. In the case of McDonald's, it's the "McRib" sandwich. In the case of a beauty salon, it might be a free facial. In the case of auto repair, it could be an upgraded sound system when repairs are over $2,500.

"Uniqueness" is achievable in any market. Avis tried to beat Hertz by proclaiming "We're number two!" But Enterprise did overtake Hertz by delivering rental cars and picking them up at customer's homes. A local dry-cleaning service picks up and delivers at the commuter train station during rush hours in both directions.

The Accelerant Curve

Easy entry & large qty

Tough entry & Small qty

Competitive

Distinct

Breakthrough

Relationship & Trust = Speed of Acceleration

Newsletters / Articles / Reports / Podcasts / Check lists / blog = Free

Booklets / Books / eBooks

Live Teleseminars / Webinars

Digital Products MP3 CD DVD

Speaking

Hosting & Yr. Maint

Remote Mentoring

Mentor Program

Workshops

Newsletters

Blogs

Forums

Core Sites

Advance Sites

Million Dollar Web Sites

Alan & The Gang

Impersonal & Low Price

Personal & High Price

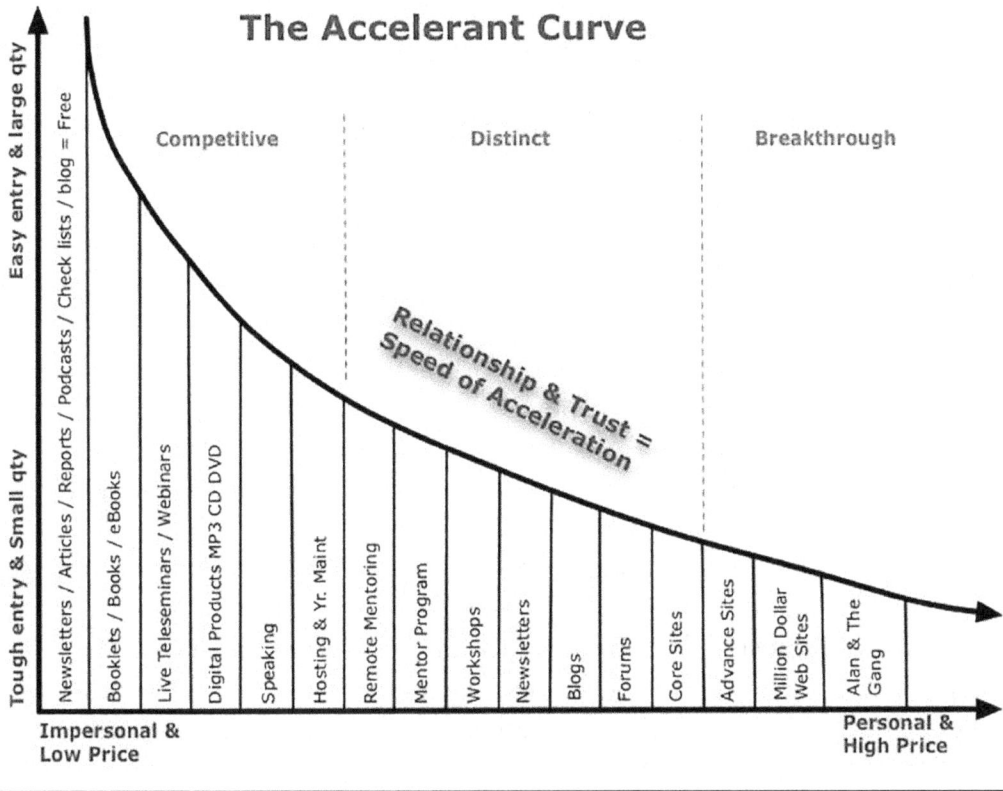

Figure 6.2   The accelerant curve.
© *Alan Weiss 2024*

What are your "uniquenesses" with your customers and clients?

Takeaways

Incorporating personalization and focusing on the customer experience are not just strategies for retention: They are essential components of a modern, customer-centric business model that can drive sustained success and growth.

Engagement and Communication

Active communication allows for real-time feedback from customers. This immediate insight can be invaluable for quickly addressing concerns and improving your offerings. You do have to discriminate, however, between promotion and value to the customer. Engagement isn't about "upselling" or reminding people you have a sale or urging people to try a new product or service.

Engagement is about providing information and value *as if the recipient were not your customer!* A propane company or a generator supplier might send a newsletter monthly with tips about how best to insulate and weatherproof a home. A software company can advise on what to do in order to restore the internet after a power failure, and how to purchase and utilize surge suppressors.

Police and fire companies often provide bulletins and articles on how to prevent burglaries and fires. They heighten this during the holidays. "Engage" means to "occupy, involve, or attract." Think of this as a conversation with customers (and prospects) and not a sales approach.

"Do good and good will follow."

These actions have very long-term implications because they foster trust through transparency.

Open and honest communication fosters trust. Trust is a critical component of customer retention because clients need to feel confident in your ability to manage their resources wisely. A trusting customer will always give you the benefit of the doubt, accepting human error, and never attributing nefarious motives to mistakes. But an untrusting customer won't be a customer for long, seeing patterns of deceit and deliberate errors.

Through engagement and communication, you can provide valuable information and education to your customers. This not only adds value, but also empowers customers to make informed decisions, which enhances satisfaction and loyalty. When you add education, you create a more discerning and sophisticated consumer who will *not* simply judge offers by price, but will search for true value and ROI irrespective of price.

We talked earlier of the emotional ties to brands which prompt people to spend more to "belong" to the higher status entity. Once trust is present, many consumers equate high price with quality. That is, instead of price following higher value, it's believed that higher price *implies higher value*. You can see that in Figure 6.3.

Many people look at virtually identical products and services from different sources—hammers, tax services, office supplies—and often assume the higher-priced options are qualitatively better than the others. Why buy a possibly less effective tax service when a few dollars more per hour will

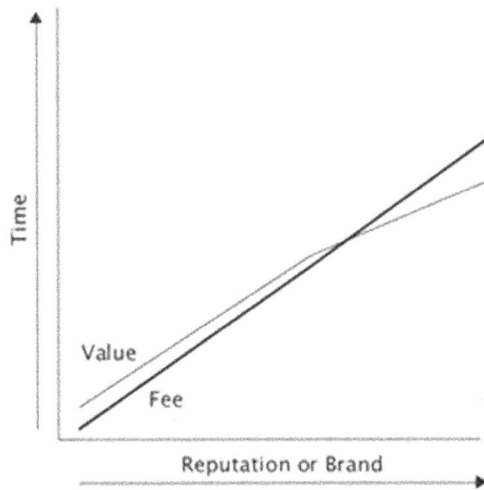

Figure 6.3   Value following fee.

Source: **The Consulting Bible,** *Alan Weiss, Wiley, 2021.*

provide better quality? And during the pandemic, many companies survived by *raising their prices* as "special pandemic offers."

Effective communication strategies can inform customers about additional products or services that meet their needs. This may encourage further investment in your brand. "Effective" means two things:

- Not too often; not too infrequently. A monthly newsletter is fine, a daily email is not.
- The value is the point, not a promotion.

Consistent engagement through various communication channels ensures your brand remains top-of-mind. When customers need a service or product you offer, they're more likely to choose your brand over others. Consumer sales (and B2B sales) are all about timing, and consistent engagement keeps your brand and value in front of customers when needs arise.

By engaging with customers across their preferred communication channels—whether it's email, social media, or direct messaging—you meet them where they are. This helps to enhance the overall customer experience. Great salespeople don't sit with a phone waiting for it to ring. They "hit the streets" (or the computer). The same should apply to your business.

Takeaways

Incorporating strategic engagement and communication into your customer retention efforts strengthens relationships with existing customers. It also sets the foundation for sustainable growth and success over the long haul and through turbulent times.

Notes

1 https://hbr.org/2014/10/the-value-of-keeping-the-right-customers
2 This is also the basis for the unethical "pyramid schemes" and "multi-level marketing" efforts that provide members with commissions for simply bringing on more members to try to make commissions without any substantial product or service sales at all.
3 Total days to cash (TDTC). Blog Post by Alan Weiss, "Business of Consulting," October 7, 2020, alanweiss.com, reprinted with permission.
4 *Value Based Fees*, Alan Weiss, John Wiley, 2021.

Chapter 7

Innovation and Adaptation

Cultivating a Culture of Innovation

Promote an environment where ideas are freely shared, and communication flows across all levels of the organization. Open dialogue fosters collaboration and the exchange of innovative ideas.

For example, make intrinsic information extrinsic, and extrinsic information intrinsic.

- **Intrinsic Information:** That which is known to an individual, but not necessarily to others.
- **Extrinsic Information:** That which is known by the organization, but not necessarily to all those who need it.

Hence, individual workers need to share information and best practices with others who may need it. For example, a salesperson reports that it's easy to sell a warranty before the product is purchased, and this information is then shared by the organization with all relevant people. Conversely, the organization learns of a key defect that might have to be corrected in certain products and shares that information with all call center members. This prevents individuals from having to "reinvent the wheel" or tell customers they'll have to get back to them after some investigation.[1]

Ideas and new approaches need to be shared and evaluated for applicability, not critiqued—especially not critiqued because of the source,

DOI: 10.4324/9781003616597-8

or "that's not your job." Customer-facing people are the ideal sources of new ideas.

Equip your staff with the tools, time, and resources they need to explore new ideas and to experiment. This support can significantly boost their ability to innovate. Recognize that there are three kinds of innovation:

- **Opportunism:** Something occurs which triggers a positive and profitable action, no matter how temporary. If a parade is suddenly scheduled to march by your hotel, raise the prices of the rooms facing the route. If the state demands "hands-free only" phone use in cars, create and sell adapters that can use the existing beverage holders.
- **Conformist Innovation:** Uber is merely a sophisticated taxi service. It didn't invent third-party transport, but it did pioneer extensive technology for scheduling and hailing, clean vehicles, language-fluent drivers, and different classes of service (including infants, handicapped, and animals).
- **Nonconformist Innovation:** This is the truly new, such as powered flight or television. The greatest example of our age is probably Amazon, a massively successful distribution service for a huge amount of products and services (recently including telehealth), delivered rapidly.

PERSEVERANCE PRESSURE

Survival is based on growth. Growth is based on innovation. And innovation is based on the right behaviors, not solely victories—the "freedom to fail" is essential.

Invest in training and development programs that keep your team updated on the latest trends, technologies, and methodologies. This investment will encourage continuous growth and innovation. But make sure these programs aren't simply "getting a ticket stamped" without a clear increase in subsequent job performance.

The keys to *effectiveness* in training are:

- Clear objectives and business outcomes to be met (not "better communication," but rather "better communication to rapidly deliver new products."

- Clear metrics of success (not "attend three training programs" but "new products are now delivered in half the time").
- If an "outside" firm delivers this, ensure you have references and a design specific for you, not a cookie-cutter program they sell.
- Given the above, assess the return on your investment. It must be in excess of 10:1.

As discussed earlier, ensure that intrinsic and extrinsic learning—both from training and from on-the-job experience—are transferred throughout your business.

While fostering creativity, it's also important to have clear objectives and expectations regarding innovation. This clarity helps focus efforts and aligns innovation with business goals. As we've noted, innovation is not a project; it's a philosophy and belief. It needs to be a part of the work environment on a daily basis.

Encourage employees to recommend changes or new techniques. If a teller points out that the bank can inform people of relevant products most effectively when interacting at the teller's station, provide brochures and applications as handouts. If a salesperson points out that almost all of the new business she receives originates with referrals from happy customers, consider a reward for referrals, and a larger one for referrals that result in business.

Acknowledge and reward both the big breakthroughs and the small improvements. Recognition not only motivates the innovator but also inspires others to think creatively. As we've stated, you need to reward the *behaviors,* not just the "successes," so that the behaviors are constant.

Design work environments that facilitate collaboration and spontaneous exchanges. These can include open office layouts, communal areas, and digital collaboration platforms. Encourage people to talk to each other. (When I started my banking career as a credit analyst, we were chastised for talking on the job!) People learning together fosters innovation.

Leadership should actively participate in and demonstrate commitment to the innovation process. Leaders who challenge the status quo and encourage experimentation influence their teams to do the same. No one believes what they read or hear in organizations; they only believe what they *see.* What examples are you providing for them to demonstrate your commitment to innovation and positive change?

Here's a hint: Don't start sentences with "That would never work here... ."

Develop processes for capturing, evaluating, and implementing ideas from all levels of the organization. An effective idea management system ensures that valuable insights don't get lost and are acted upon. Keep a log or a journal and follow up on what's been done, and why things are progressing or not. Many organizations have a visible timeline or map of ideas in progress and explaining why something didn't work is as important as explaining why something did.

Takeaway

By focusing on these key areas, organizations can cultivate a culture that values innovation and actively practices it and encourages it.

Embracing Adaptability

Encourage an organizational culture that views challenges as opportunities to learn and grow, rather than obstacles to success. This mindset is key to adaptability. And it thrives in resilience.

None of us is successful all the time, largely because the best plans are often undone by surprising competitive actions, regulatory changes, technological advances, consumer normative pressure, and poor assumptions. Resilience is about "bouncing forward" and not "falling back and recovering." In Figure 7.1 you can see an example.

The traits on the left are consistent with what we've been discussing throughout the book to this point:

- Recognition of success: Proper metrics
- Positive self-talk: Seeing opportunities, not threats
- Healthy feedback intolerance: The customer is not always right
- Dynamically growing skillsets: Training and innovative behaviors
- Social cue adeptness: Being opportunistic
- Judgment: Intrinsic/extrinsic information and knowledge sharing

Consequently, employees' judgment improves, leading to success and reinforcement. However, when obstacles arise, these traits lead to quick recovery and advancement towards success. You may be delayed, but you're not derailed.

Resilience

Setback

Success!

contingent reserve

**Your Decisions
and Behavior**

**Trust in Your
Judgment**

Recognition of success
Positive self-talk
Healthy feedback intolerance
Appropriate avatars
Dynamically growing skillset
Social cue adeptness
Judgment (principle/taste)

Your defined
future

Constant navigation

Critical gyroscope

Seven Fuel Tanks
(Hyper-traits)

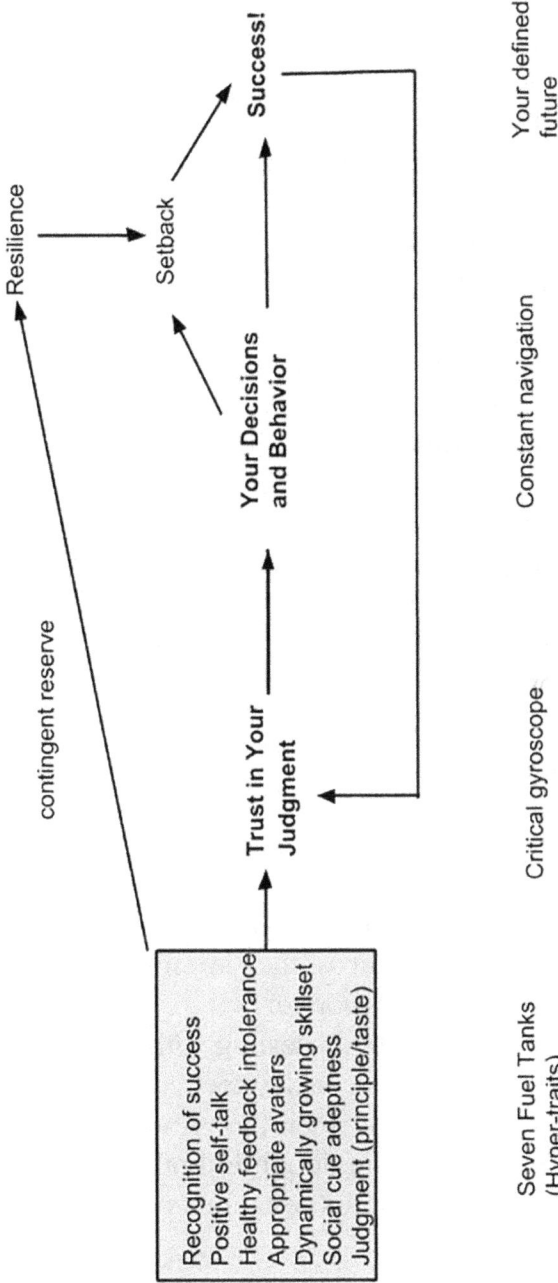

Figure 7.1 Resilience.

Source: The Resilience Advantage: Stop Managing Stress and Find Your Resilience, Richard Citrin and Alan Weiss, Business Expert Press, 2016.

Implement flexible work processes that can easily be adjusted as circumstances change. This flexibility allows the organization to respond quickly to new opportunities or threats. You should include cross-training, a "Plan B" for critical processes (the equivalent of a generator if the main power fails), and quick priority-setting for the issues of greatest impact.

Flexible work processes include what has become the great debate about remote work and "hybrid" employees. Keep in mind that, even in an office environment, *no one is working and productive for a full 40-hour week.* There is down time, wasted time, interrupted time, and so forth. There's no empirical evidence—no studies—that show presence in an office is more productive than remote work.

Be flexible in terms of what you expect and consequently plan to do. The metrics we've raised periodically certainly fit here: Are remote employees producing the results you are expecting of them, especially compared to employees in the office? If so, why change anything? If not, find the cause, which may not be the location so much as poor communications.

Regularly provide training and development opportunities that enable employees to acquire new skills and knowledge. The training will make it easier for your team to adapt to new roles or technologies. As noted, ensure the training is oriented toward business outcomes and results, not mere attendance at courses, whether internal or external.

Encourage collaboration between different departments and teams. Cross-functional teams can bring diverse perspectives and solutions to challenges which will enhance the organization's ability to adapt. *One great mechanism for such collaboration is to always include people in meetings from other departments and include people in teams from other disciplines.* If the R&D people share joint experiences, they are much less likely to blame the other units or to fail to collaborate.

This can even extend to client visits or dealing with customers on site. Too many "back office" people never actually meet customers. But people who interface with clients and customers tend to remember names and faces and always give the benefit of the doubt: in both directions. It's amazing to me how bartenders in various restaurants remember the favorite drinks of so many different customers!

Keep abreast of the latest trends and developments in your industry. Being proactive rather than reactive to changes can give your business a competitive edge. Read extensively (not on social media)—industry journals, professional magazines, the *Wall Street Journal*, and the local news that your customer base is most likely to read and hear.

Empower employees to make decisions and take action without always seeking approval from higher-ups. Autonomy can speed up response times and encourage a more adaptable workforce. In Figure 7.2 you'll see some of the differences.

Set aside time to regularly review organizational goals and strategies. Make adjustments as needed to stay aligned with the changing environment. Include and involve your people as goals shift, emphasizing what is needed from them and what you can provide for them.

Takeaway

By prioritizing these practices, organizations can build a culture of adaptability. This will ensure they remain resilient and competitive no matter what challenges or opportunities arise.

Strategies for Implementing Change

Start by clearly defining what the change is and what you aim to achieve with it. Clear objectives will guide the implementation process and help measure success. Here are some guidelines:

■ Indicate how the change is in the best interests of employees and/or customers. People are most likely to change when they perceive *it's in their best interests to do so.*

Power vs. Powerlessness	
Powerless	Empowered
■ Create bureaucracy	■ Do the right thing
■ Are insecure	■ Are self-confident
■ See "them and us"	■ See "we"
■ Focus on task	■ Focus on result
■ Focus rules	■ Think
■ CYA	■ Take risks
■ See win/loss issues	■ See win/win issues

Figure 7.2   Powerless and empowered.

- People usually look to a new future with anticipation and happiness, *but they fear the journey.* Show them how you intend to lead them there (and remember the resilience discussion earlier).
- Ensure that *all* relevant stakeholders are involved, which might include suppliers, creditors, investors, and so forth.
- A strategy is a vision of the future, not the tactics to get there. *Ensure commitment to the "what" before discussing the "how."*

How you institute change may involve many people, but *whether you institute it* is a strictly leadership decision.

Create a detailed plan that outlines the steps needed to implement the change, including timelines, resources required, and key personnel involved. A well-structured plan provides a roadmap for the change process. This is the "how." Always include risks. You can't avoid them, so plan to try to prevent problems *as well as mitigate their impact if they do occur.* For example, you need safe wiring and separation of combustibles, *as well as* insurance and sprinklers.

Implement gradually if timing permits. If possible, implement the change in phases rather than all at once. This phased approach allows for adjustments based on feedback and can make the transition more manageable for everyone involved. It will also make people more comfortable as the "journey" is undertaken and they feel safe and in control. Also, if something goes wrong, it only impacts that phase and not the entire project, and it is far more easily correctable.

Of course, some change has to be streamlined and accelerated: natural disasters (pandemic), new technologies (AI), competitive actions (new services and products), and social norms (trends and influencers). The fashion industry is often embroiled in this. Timing is everything, because you can wind up with an out-of-date inventory or an untested one—both of which are potentially deadly.

Refer to our earlier discussions about sampling customers, asking for their input and experiences. Focus on your best customers first, those you want to retain at all costs.

Continuously monitor the implementation process and be prepared to make adjustments based on what is working and what is not. Flexibility is key to overcoming unforeseen challenges.

When you're hiking and come across a small rock in the path, you don't treat it as a boulder—you move it or go around it. If you're traveling and face cancellations or tie-ups, you don't abandon your plans; you use a backup or a detour.

This applies to your innovations and adaptations, as well. Don't allow people to see a small blemish and turn it into a fatal disease. Never assume that people will have the same discipline, accountability, and energy that you do. Create oversight so that you can keep things in perspective for people and assist when a change of plans is justifiably required.

But detours are still intended to get you to your original destination, not a different one. Plan B is designed to take over from Plan A but proceed to the same endpoint. Too many plans and improvements are abandoned as soon as *any* resistance is felt. You have to keep people's eyes on the destination. No one can plan properly looking in the rear-view mirror or at the wake of the ship.

Remember, wind is not helpful to your sailboat if you don't know your port-of-call.

Recognize and celebrate milestones as the change is implemented. Acknowledging achievements can boost morale and motivate the team to continue pushing forward. We've spoken of not rewarding "only victories" but also the right behaviors, even if the goals weren't achieved. Similarly, find ways to reward "progress points." Don't wait for some finality: Celebrate progress. *Athletes celebrate good plays well before the game is decided.*

Understand that resistance is a natural part of the change process. Listen to concerns, provide clear explanations, and address issues constructively to move forward.

Consensus is something people can live with, not something they're willing to die for!

Try to mediate different points of view, especially from your top lieutenants whose behavior will influence their subordinates. Arrive at compromise: Combine positive elements of different approaches. Come up with a third or fourth alternative that suits most people most of the time. Remember that the "what" and the "why" are the leadership, strategic decisions, but the "how" is open to good ideas and innovative approaches.

The sequence is hugely important, because people have to know the destination (your destinations) before they can intelligently contribute to the routes to arrive there. What you cannot afford is the belief that they can change the route. If you don't make the tough strategic decisions, then no one will, because no one else is empowered to do so!

After the change has been implemented, evaluate the process and outcomes. Identify what worked well and what could be improved for future changes. Learning from each experience strengthens the organization's capacity for change. It will also accustom people to the necessity and possible rapidity of change as a way of life, not an exception.

Takeaway

These strategies can help ensure that the process of implementing change is as smooth and effective as possible. This will lead to sustained growth and innovation within your business.

Fostering a Responsive Business Model

Encourage continuous learning and development to keep skills sharp and ideas fresh, enabling your team to adapt quickly to new challenges.

You want to develop an environment that attracts and retains talented people who have positive mindsets. Bear in mind that people don't leave organizations because they are unhappy; they leave bosses for whom they do not want to continue working. Thus, people have to feel comfortable raising ideas or challenging current practices; they need the "freedom to fail," and they require proactive involvement.

This can't be a "special" project or a brief focus; it has to be a way of life in the organization. Figure 7.3 illustrates the importance:

1 = Procrastination and delay
2 = Uninspired Effort

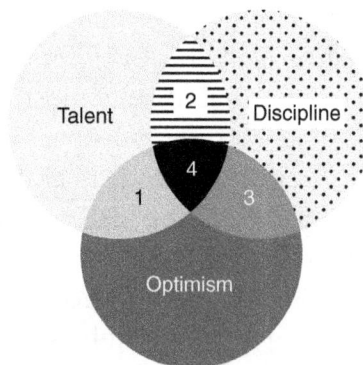

Figure 7.3   Talent and environment.

3 = Poor Results
4 = The True Motivated and Productive Employee

You need all three elements and an environment which creates and fosters them.

Adopt flexible work policies to attract and retain top talent, fostering a more adaptable and innovative workforce. The huge issue at this writing is that of workers' locations: in the office, remote, or a combination thereof (hybrid). Some suggestions:

- Customer-interacting should be on-site or on the customer's site: Tellers, repair people, realty agents, retail store sales.
- Customer support people can be remote: Call center operators, schedulers, technicians, travel agents.

However, since leaders usually promote or select people for key assignments *based upon personal interactions and experiences in different company environments,* it's important for the employee and manager/owner to arrange for such interactions so as not to put anyone at the disadvantage of "out of sight, out of mind," and to ensure the best quality selections.

It may well be that "hybrid" is effective if handled correctly, and solely remote is for only people intent on and content with doing a single job repeatedly. Perhaps part-time and subcontractors are best suited for this: People who don't foresee or desire higher levels of responsibility within the firm.

One final observation about a myth: NO ONE works a 40-hour week, even if rooted to a chair in an office. There is wasted time, communing with employees, and useless meetings. So, distractions at home may be real, but so are distractions in the office! Measure people on the *results they produce against your metrics and expectations.* At this writing, many private companies and governmental agencies are forcing people back into the office full-time. That is a task, not a result.

Clearly define and regularly revisit your value proposition to ensure it remains relevant and compelling in a changing market. The value proposition is how people think you can improve their condition. It has to be compelling and "other-oriented." A value proposition is similar to a mission statement, and involves *why* your business exists, and *what* it intends to accomplish *for customers and clients.*

On a large scale, pharmaceutical giant Merck's mission has always been "to bring state-of-the-art health research to the greatest areas of human health needs." On a smaller scale, an accounting firm might have "to create financial security and confidence in business and personal pursuits to our clients." Notice that this focus accomplishes:

- A clear understanding of improvement and "what's in it for me" with buyers and prospects.
- An employee focus on the intent of their jobs (people may join venture capital firms to grow rich, but they don't join Merck to grow rich).
- The correct metrics to judge performance—getting to work on time is not as important as filing tax returns that protect a client from legal challenges.
- Higher customer satisfaction—customers are unaware of internal metrics and guidelines and who is meeting or not meeting them. They are concerned about their own well-being—is my cleaning done without harmful chemicals, without damage, and returned on time? Does the grill I purchased operate correctly, without danger of fire, and prepare food to the proper levels?

Obviously, while Merck's value proposition and that of the accounting firm may not need to change over time, you may still choose to revisit yours regularly. If you're in an industry or market subject to volatility and disruption—real estate, auto, insurance, hospitality, entertainment, and so forth—you may find the need to change your focus to suit the bullet points above. Netflix has done this, but the postal service never has (or they'd be leaders in email and overnight package delivery).

Encourage calculated (prudent) risk-taking and view failures as learning opportunities, creating a culture that supports innovation and adaptation. This is another issue where you can lead by example, acknowledging errors and bad decisions on your part when appropriate, and indicating to others what you learned from them and how you'll be improved from it.

Never shy away from apologizing in public.

And stick to empirical evidence and observed behavior, not belittlement. If you ask someone why they're chronically 15 minutes late to a meeting, you may find out that their childcare responsibilities have changed or there's extensive roadwork being done along their commute route. But telling them they're "not a team player" or irresponsible is not the example you want to set, and it's not a behavior that's going to support risk taking and "the freedom to fail."

And the freedom to fail—once—is not freedom.

Takeaway

Incorporating these strategies into your business model can significantly enhance your ability to respond to changes and foster a culture of innovation and adaptability.

Note

1 For further information on this process, see *The Knowledge Creating Company*, Ikujiro Nonaka and Hirotaka Takeuchi, Oxford University Press (1995).

Chapter 8

Managing Stress and Burnout

Identifying Signs of Stress and Burnout

The sensation that one's responsibilities or circumstances are too much to handle, leading to feelings of being swamped or defeated, is often called "overwhelm" or "burnout." But these are simply handy slogans applied to very serious problems.

As an overview, Figure 8.1 shows the relationship between doing something which creates high interest—call it "passion"—and the importance of doing something of importance to others (think here of your customers, clients, and the general community).

For you and for your employees, you need "fulfillment," where you are passionate about what value you provide and that value is of high importance. If the value is of importance, but there is little interest in it from employees (or you, or your family), you have merely a daily "grind," AKA: a nine-to-five job.

When you do love doing something but it's of low importance, then it's probably a hobby or addiction. Many of us are "addicted" to video games, or candy, or sports. But some addictions are with alcohol or drugs or food. Finally, when we're engaged in the unimportant and we're bored, then we're simply indifferent.

"Motivation" is about helping people become passionate about what they do, and it only comes from within.

 DOI: 10.4324/9781003616597-9

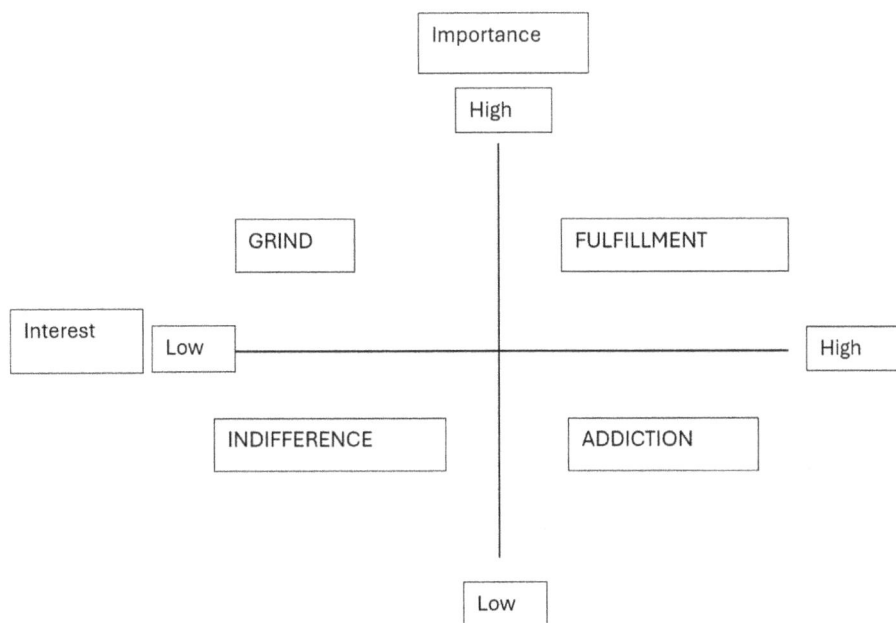

Figure 8.1 Importance and interest.

Source: **Building Dynamic Business Communities,** *Alan Weiss, Routledge, 2025.*

PERSEVERANCE PRESSURE

Motivation is intrinsic. You can't motivate someone else, but you can create an environment and a relationship that tends to foster others' self-motivation.

Constant fatigue is a sign of "burnout." Persistent tiredness or exhaustion that doesn't improve with rest makes it difficult to carry out daily tasks, or be innovative, or to perform well. This will tell you that you don't have a "skills" problem, but rather a health problem.

Let me point out here that you should learn the signs of clinical depression for yourself, your family, and your employees. People may be "depressed," that is, sad or unhappy, and get over it. But clinical depression is an illness and needs medical treatment. Here are some indicators:

▪ Continuous low mood or sadness.
▪ Feeling hopeless and helpless.
▪ Having low self-esteem.

- ▪ Feeling tearful.
- ▪ Feeling guilt-ridden.
- ▪ Feeling irritable and intolerant of others.
- ▪ Having no motivation or interest in things.
- ▪ Finding it difficult to make decisions.
- ▪ Inability to sleep.
- ▪ Lack of interest in former hobbies and pastimes.
- ▪ Decreased romantic and sexual interest.[1]

Minor annoyances may cause disproportionate frustration or anger, affecting relationships with colleagues, friends, and family. When you see irrational outbursts of argument, accusation, or even physical violence, you may be seeing Intermittent Explosive Disorder (IED). On the highways, this is "road rage," but at work or at home it's "life rage." This, too, requires professional intervention.[2]

A noticeable decline in enthusiasm and satisfaction in work or daily activities can occur, where tasks that were once enjoyable now feel burdensome. This can be the result of cognitive difficulties, which may unexpectedly occur due to illness, trauma, or stress. Experiencing trouble with concentration, memory, or decision-making, making it hard to perform at usual standards, is an immediate indicator and should be investigated. Make sure your communication lines are open and candid, because this often can occur unbeknownst to the individual while no one is comfortable pointing it out.

Physical symptoms can be headaches, muscle tension, gastrointestinal problems, or other stress-related physical issues. Stress is a major cause of more serious illnesses. We all suffer from distress at times, but the answer isn't in trying to eliminate stress, but to manage it. There is a "good" stress—eustress—which enables people to perform better under deadlines or other pressures, as shown in Figure 8.2.

You can see that when stress is very low, productivity also tends to be low, because there are no consequences for poor productivity. But when stress is very high, people become "paralyzed" with fear, and productivity also plummets. In between, however, is the "eustress," the stress that creates adrenaline and the eagerness to get things done fast and well.

Too often, leaders see low productivity because of low negative consequences, and increase the consequences so severely that they drive people immediately to the right edge, *which maintains the low productivity*

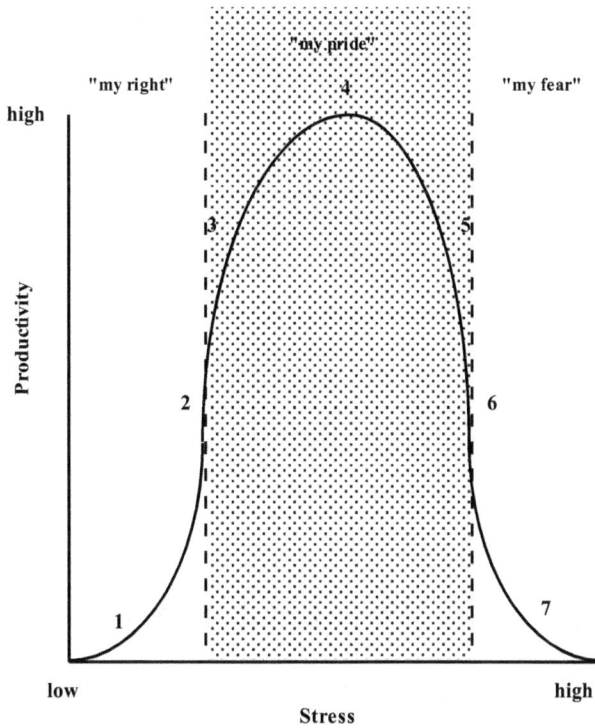

Figure 8.2 Stress and productivity.

because the stress is never correctly managed to remain tolerable and "in the middle."

You might find people withdrawing from social interactions, work engagements, or family activities, and feeling disconnected from others. Don't be too urgent in taking action, since this can be caused, short-term, by physical illness, disappointment, bad news, even a favorite team losing a playoff game!

However, if it persists over the course of a week or more, it's time to look into the causes and make sure that this is not being caused by something in the environment, the organization, or a mental health issue.

Turning to alcohol, drugs, excessive eating, or other unhealthy behaviors as a way to cope with stress or emotional pain is a dead giveaway—especially if this has originated recently. These are unhealthy coping mechanisms which are usually easily detected. The key is to find their cause, not to assess blame or critique. It doesn't improve things to say, "You've gained a few pounds," or "Why are you drinking so much at lunch?"

but it can help to say, "I notice you're increasing your food consumption. Is that deliberate, or are you unaware of it?"

Ignoring personal needs, such as proper nutrition, physical activity, and adequate rest, can lead to a decline in overall well-being or be a symptom. One day with a stain on clothing is something that happens to all of us. But wearing the same outfit daily, unkempt hair, unpleasant odors, and so forth usually indicate some form of mild or clinical depression.

Takeaway
Recognizing these signs early can help individuals take proactive steps to manage stress and prevent burnout. It's important to seek support, whether through professional help, lifestyle changes, or collegial strategies aimed at reducing stress and improving well-being.

Creating a Supportive Work Environment

Encourage employees to express their ideas, concerns, and feelings openly without fear of judgment or retaliation. Regular check-ins and feedback sessions can facilitate this. Here are some options, depending on the size of your firm:

- Have breakfast with employees on-site, and casually discuss working conditions, customer questions, and what's working well and what can be improved. (Recall our "intrinsic/extrinsic" discussion earlier in the book.)
- Chat with employees at their workstations. Go with a salesperson to a client. Stop people in the halls and ask how they're doing.
- Use outside resources to run focus groups, which are confidential and oriented toward certain issues, e.g., the work environment, equipment condition, customer complaints, personal time policies, and so forth. These groups tend to "self-sanction," in that members will point out falsehoods that others may raise.
- Use outside resources for one-on-one interviews, which are confidential and encourage personal concerns to be raised.
- Provide the means for anonymous suggestions and feedback.
- Provide a periodic newsletter about company progress in ongoing projects, new clients, repair issues, and employee family matters (children graduating, awards, community service, and so forth).

Acknowledge the hard work and achievements of team members. Recognition can be as simple as a thank-you note or as significant as rewards for outstanding contributions. Keep in mind that money is not a motivator (although the absence of money is a demotivator), but that recognition for one's contributions and agency (empowerment, latitude of action) is a very important motivational factor.

Hence, consider the following:

- **Offer Flexibility:** Where possible, provide flexible working hours or the option to work from home. Flexibility helps employees manage their work-life balance more effectively. It also accommodates childcare and educational demands on time.
- **Provide Professional Development Opportunities:** Invest in the growth of your team by offering training, workshops, or courses that help them advance their skills and careers. These don't have to be strictly work-related, e.g., financial planning, tax preparation, writing skills.
- **Encourage Regular Breaks:** Promote a culture where taking short, regular breaks throughout the day is normal. Breaks help reduce mental fatigue and boost productivity. Allow conversational talk among people.
- **Foster Team Collaboration and Support:** Encourage teamwork and create opportunities for employees to support each other. A collaborative environment can reduce feelings of isolation and increase job satisfaction. Consider an occasional "bring your kid to work" day, or even, "bring your pet to work" day (if safety and environment permit).
- **Implement Stress Management Resources:** Offer resources such as workshops on stress management techniques, access to counseling services, or subscriptions to mindfulness apps. (Example: Share the bell curve chart in this chapter about how to handle stress effectively.)
- **Ensure Workload is Realistic:** Regularly review workloads to ensure they are manageable. Overloading employees can lead to stress and burnout, so it's important to adjust expectations and deadlines as necessary.
- **Create a Healthy Physical Environment:** Invest in ergonomic office furniture, ensure adequate lighting, and provide access to healthy snacks or a relaxation area. A comfortable and healthy workplace can significantly reduce stress.

■ **Lead by Example:** Leadership should model healthy work habits and behaviors, such as taking breaks, respecting boundaries, and prioritizing well-being. This sets a positive tone for the entire organization. Demonstrate "fitness" physically, intellectually, and emotionally.

Takeaway

By implementing these strategies, businesses can create a more supportive and nurturing work environment that helps employees thrive even in the face of challenges.

Implementing Effective Time Management

Break larger projects into smaller, manageable tasks with clear, achievable goals. Setting and meeting smaller milestones can reduce overwhelm and increase motivation. If you intend to "clear out the garage," the chances are that the enormity of that task will undermine your energy to actually do it. But if you intend to "clear three shelves and throw out the old paint cans," that will more likely get done.

"Effective" is often "incremental."

Also, don't be hesitant to combine personal and business tasks. You can go to the bank, the post office, pick up your cleaning, and have lunch on one trip.

Identify the most critical tasks and tackle them first. Use a system to categorize tasks by seriousness, urgency, and growth. It's also a good idea to try to handle the most difficult or distasteful tasks earlier in the day so that they don't "cast a cloud" on you during the day. (A great many people work out early in the morning because they don't like to be facing it all day if they work out in the evening, and they're more prone to finding some excuse to cancel.)

If you have a priority of collecting overdue payments, make the calls or write the letters first thing in the morning. (You'll also improve your chances of collecting by getting noticed early.) If you have to deal with an unhappy customer, do it early while you're fresh and energetic.

When you establish what these priorities should be, here's a litmus test:

■ **Seriousness:** How important is the issue? Does it have major consequences, or is it a minor annoyance?

- **Urgency:** How fast must I move to avoid further pain or achieve more immediate improvement? Should I drop everything else, schedule it for later on, or get to it when I can?
- **Growth:** Left alone, is the issue stable, getting better, or getting worse? If the latter two, at what rate? Does it make sense to use "watchful waiting"?

Keep track of deadlines, appointments, and tasks with a planner or digital scheduling tool. This helps visualize how your time is allocated and assists in planning ahead. While digital calendars and diaries and automated appointments are in vogue, just keep in mind that the only way to see a full year or even a month at one glance is to use hard copy.

That might be a Filofax® or other paper option, or a large wall calendar in your office or workspace. But it's important to see "side-by-side" so that you don't schedule meetings that are back-to-back, or issues that might well run longer than you anticipate with a sudden arbitrary cutoff for the next task. This is also true for vacations and recreation. Don't leave work or return to it immediately before or after vacations. Give yourself a day or so to acclimate. The business hasn't collapsed in your absence and won't the next time, either.

Create consistent daily routines to structure your day. Having a routine can increase efficiency and reduce the time spent deciding what to do next. Some people make themselves coffee and breakfast or go out to a coffee shop to chat with regular morning acquaintances. Some watch or listen to the news. Others check overnight email arrivals.

A routine (that allows for exceptions at times) creates a "steadiness" to begin the day. And it can and should include getting the kids off to school, walking the dogs, or reading something pleasant (comics, sports pages). It may be Wordle or a crossword puzzle. Start your day positive, happy, and "familiar." Music and comedy recordings are also great alternatives.

Focus on one task at a time. Multitasking can reduce the quality of work and increase stress levels. Single-tasking improves focus and productivity. It's been shown that multitasking decreases the quality of each of the tasks involved. While multitasking is commonly perceived as a means to accomplish more in less time, it often does more harm than good. The truth is most multitasking is a myth that hampers our ability to focus and perform tasks effectively.[3]

Delegate when possible—share responsibilities with others when appropriate. Delegating tasks can lighten your workload and provide others with growth opportunities. There's an old saying which goes, "When someone enters your office never let them leave anything on your desk. Insist that they take something from your desk with them when they leave."

Delegation can apply to suppliers and customers, as well as to your employees. Airline remote boarding passes and kiosks where people print their own luggage tags are examples, as is advance ordering in everything from high-end restaurants to Dunkin' Donuts.

Identify what commonly distracts you and take steps to minimize these interruptions. This might involve turning off notifications, setting specific times to check emails, or creating a dedicated additional workspace. If you must play a video game to relieve the tension, schedule it for 30 minutes and set an alarm when the time is up. Never promise anyone "instant access" to you, but rather promise "quick responsiveness" when the timing is best for you.

Regularly review how you spend your time and adjust your strategies as needed. Being flexible and willing to change your approach can help you find what works best for you. Keep a journal over two weeks, using categories such as:

- Marketing
- Customer discussions
- Employee discussions
- Supplier discussions
- Meetings of any kind
- R&D discussions
- Performance evaluations
- Financial management
- Legal issues

You get the idea. Use two weeks to ensure exceptions don't distort the overall results. Then ask yourself if you're spending sufficient time on the right priorities. And here's a hint: You're probably already in far too many meetings, which are good for taking action, but terrible for merely exchanging information.

Takeaway
Implementing these time management strategies can help create a more balanced, productive work environment that supports mental well-being and reduces the risk of stress and burnout.

Setting Boundaries and Learning to Say No

Understand your limits and needed boundaries. Reflect on your physical, emotional, and mental limits. Recognizing these will help you identify when you need to set boundaries. Say "no" without the need for justification. "No, I'm busy this week" will likely result in the other person saying, "Okay, what about next week." Simply say "no," and if further questioned, "it's a personal decision."

Be direct and clear when communicating your boundaries. Use "I" statements to express your needs respectfully and assertively. Use "We" when the subject or need is properly everyone's. "Transparency" is important to reveal the "Why" behind requests or procedures that others might not appreciate are needed.

If saying "no" is difficult for you, start with small requests. Practice builds confidence, making it easier to handle larger requests over time. "No, I can't take five minutes at the moment, sorry." That really doesn't require explanation.

You can always offer alternatives and options. When saying "no," if possible, offer an alternative solution or compromise. This shows you're still supportive, even if you can't meet the original request. For example, "Why not try it yourself, first?" or "Have you asked your colleagues if it's a good idea?"

Make self-care a priority. Recognize that setting boundaries is a form of self-care. It's not selfish; it's necessary for maintaining your well-being. The "oxygen mask rule" applies: Help yourself before trying to help others. If you're mentally and emotionally prepared you'll provide better advice, be more tolerant, and find more compassion.

Regularly assess your commitments and how they align with your values and goals. This can help you decide when to say yes and when to say no. Be kind to yourself, practice self-compassion, *and forgive yourself when you make an error.* Fix it if you can. Apologize if you can. Learn from it. Then move on. Don't dwell on the error: Focus on the "fix."

When it's perhaps okay to provide a reason for saying no, avoid over-justifying or making excuses. This can lead to unnecessary stress and may weaken your position. Don't be interrogated and don't feel you're putting someone in a tough position just by refusing a request. As a rule, don't accept delegated work from others. Teach them to fish: Don't catch fish for them.

Understand that some people might be disappointed or upset when you set boundaries. Remember, your well-being must come first, and those who value you will respect your limits. You're not there to please; you're there to be successful and to gain trust and respect.

Limit your availability via email, social media, and messaging platforms. Set specific times to check these communications and inform others if you're unavailable outside these times. (And remember, if you are someone who is promoted, your former peers are now subordinates, and your former superiors are now peers. Make social adjustments as necessary. Be careful in whom you confide.)

Takeaway

Incorporating these strategies into your daily life can significantly reduce stress and protect against burnout. Setting boundaries and learning to say no are essential for maintaining your health, well-being, and productivity, especially during challenging times. YOU are the one primarily responsible for your own well-being.

Seeking Professional Help When Needed

Understand the symptoms of stress and burnout that may require professional help, such as prolonged sadness, anxiety, detachment, physical exhaustion, and feelings of hopelessness. (We've addressed particular signs and resources earlier.) Acknowledge that seeking help is a sign of strength, not weakness. It's an important step towards taking control of your well-being.

Familiarize yourself with the types of professionals who can offer support, such as psychologists, psychiatrists, counselors, and coaches, and understand the differences in their services. For example, a psychiatrist is a medical doctor who can prescribe drugs. A clinician is specially trained to counsel people, as opposed to someone who only holds a PhD in psychology. There are people with "coaching certifications" which are virtually meaningless. (Who "certifies" the certifiers?)

Don't hesitate to ask for recommendations from trusted friends, family members, or healthcare providers to find a professional that suits your needs. The best person to ask for such help is your personal physician who will know you well enough to choose compatible approaches and resources. (If you don't have a regular personal physician, get one!)

Ensure that the professional you choose is licensed and has relevant experience, especially in dealing with stress and burnout. For example, most "behavioral tests" offered by coaches and consultants are not validated and can provide very inaccurate responses, no better than horoscopes. However, licensed psychologists can provide highly valid testing instruments and analyses for which they've received special training.

Consider Teletherapy: If accessibility or scheduling is a concern, consider teletherapy options. Many professionals offer virtual sessions, which can be just as effective as in-person therapy. This is now being accepted under the umbrella of telehealth. No matter what approach you take, prepare well. Write down what you're experiencing, including any specific events that have contributed to your feelings of stress and burnout. This can help you articulate your needs and goals. You can also record your feelings as they occur and provide that for your therapist.

Understand that progress may be gradual. It's important to set realistic expectations and be patient with yourself throughout the process. That means you must be candid to get to matters rapidly. For therapy to be effective, it's crucial to be open and honest with your therapist. Trust in the confidentiality of the therapeutic relationship and share your thoughts and feelings freely. You must be committed to the process. Engage actively in the process and apply what you learn in therapy to your daily life. Remember, seeking help is a proactive step towards recovery and personal growth.

Finally, seek out support groups with members who have experienced and are experiencing the same feelings. You are not alone; it's part of the pressures of business ownership.

Takeaway

Seeking professional help when dealing with stress and burnout is a proactive approach to managing your mental health. It provides you with the tools and support needed to navigate challenging times more effectively.

Notes

1 For more information and detail: www.nhs.uk/mental-health/conditions/depress ion-in-adults/symptoms/

2 https://my.clevelandclinic.org/health/diseases/17786-intermittent-explosive-disorder

3 www.focuswise.com/blog/the-myth-of-multitasking#:~:text=Multitasking%20impairs%20cognitive%20function:%20When,by%20as%20much%20as%2050%25

Chapter 9

Leading Through Change and Learning from Failure

Adaptive Leadership and Visionary Thinking

Adaptive leadership is essential for navigating unpredictable market shifts and economic changes, ensuring a successful, competitive business. IBM (once International Business Machines) is a long way from being in the business of office machines, punch cards, and coding. Today, it's in the information exchange business and most of its profit comes from consulting.

The same applies to smaller businesses. The coffee shop on Main Street breaks down a wall, gets a liquor license, and has a martini bar in the evening. If there's anything more profitable than hot water and coffee beans, it's pouring vodka into a glass! The local movie theater hosts meetings, stand-up comics, and exhibitions. It provides reclining seats, hot meals, and cocktails.

All of this is possible through innovation and visionary thinking. All organizations stay in business so long as they continually grow, and they continually grow if they consistently innovate. The beauty salon adds massages, manicures, pedicures, facials, waxing, and even Pilates. It's no longer a beauty salon. Now it has become a day spa!

What can your business do that will reflect innovative growth in its products and services? Write your ideas here:

DOI: 10.4324/9781003616597-10

_____

_____

_____

_____

_____

The most adaptive leaders are always flexible. They adjust to the times.[1] Even the bureaucracy of the government can demonstrate this. When security lines became too long and slow, TSA introduced Pre-Check. For entering the US from overseas, they introduced Global Entry. These are responsive to fingerprints and retinal scans (and are even faster in many other countries). Private enterprise also entered the arena with service such as CLEAR.

Local restaurants—even high-end establishments—learned from COVID that people would gladly order and dine at home, and companies like DoorDash or Uber Eats would deliver for them, increasing profits. Suddenly, a plethora of take-out food menus jam our desk drawers and our computer email, whereas once this was solely the province of pizza, fried chicken, and Chinese food!

If necessity is the "mother of invention," then innovation is the child.

Adaptive leadership is focused on flexibility—often called "agility" in management textbooks. It's fine to have a strategy, but strategies never fail in formulation, they fail in *implementation*. This is the Mike Tyson doctrine about having a plan upon entering the boxing ring which is effective until the other guy punches you in the face.

Retail stores in New York often accommodate midnight deliveries and restocking because there is little traffic and plenty of unloading space. Some food retailers have traditional table dining, some have added drive-thru, and some now have "walk-up" windows for take-out food.

When we use GPS and find detours around traffic jams, we're demonstrating using high-tech to add to our flexibility. Some of us can still remember when we had to simply "stay the course" because getting off the main road was like wandering in the woods without a compass under a cloudy sky. (And we now use GPS on our phone even when we *walk* in new places.)

Flexibility has traditionally been represented by, "Go to plan B" when "plan A" hits a roadblock. But today we need a plan "C" and even "D." Aircraft have three or more redundant systems. The Space Shuttles had more than that, but even that didn't prevent two disasters.

Visionary thinking should drive long-term success, not just a "spurt" in the numbers. That applies to financials, but also to issues such as succession planning, new technology, new markets, and so forth. This provides the boost for individuals and teams.

It will also improve risk management in understanding and adapting to change, and provide for both preventive actions (minimizing probabilities of causes of failure) and contingent actions (minimizing the consequences of failures that inevitably do occur).

All of these benefits serve to improve morale, because the work culture is one of prudent risk and not gambling, innovation and not stodginess, looking forward and not backward. Decision-making is enhanced both by managing risk (often overlooked in decision-making) and avoidance of "paralysis by analysis." In our fast-moving world, replete with turmoil and disruption, this is more important than ever.

Finally, the sum total of visionary thinking is competitive advantage and market dominance. Instead of trying to catch up to trends, business owners and leadership *can create the trends and force others to try to catch up to them.*

Communication and Collaboration

Proactively leading change helps businesses adapt to new realities. This ensures continuity even in the face of adversity.

For example, we must build resilience. Organizations that lead change effectively are better equipped to handle future challenges. Building a culture of resilience helps to withstand market fluctuations. Resilience is about "bouncing forward" from setbacks, not reorganizing to lick wounds or defend our positions. When rapid spread of the internet threatened "Main Street" brick and mortar stores, some cut hours, prices, or staff.

But others embraced the internet, invested in the appropriate technology and expertise, and became more successful than ever, no longer "limited" to local foot traffic, but selling nationally and even globally. The Census Bureau figures for the fourth quarter of 2024, for example, indicate that $353 billion of retail sales were represented by e-commerce.[2]

Business leaders who are adept at leading change can stay ahead of industry trends and competitor movements. *Reacting to change* is insufficient, because of the time lag and the competitive advantage of those who lead the change. Restaurants which feature credit card payments at the table, with the card never out of possession of the customer, are increasingly popular (and have been standard in other countries for a long time).

A culture that embraces change is typically more dynamic, innovative, and open to new ideas. It attracts better talent and fosters a positive work environment. The old thinking was that a "skunk works" or some kind of "retreat" was necessary for innovation, as though it were a pursuit isolated from daily, routine work.

This is clearly *not* the reality. A "culture" is that set of beliefs which governs behavior. Thus, an innovative culture would foster behavior that encourages and rewards innovation on the job daily. *Incremental innovation*—a little every day—adds up to more profound change than an attempt at a "breakthrough," just as investing regularly is more profitable than trying for the "big hit" (whether in the stock market or the casinos, which can be quite similar).

The collaborative spirit can inspire three kinds of innovation:

- ▪ **Opportunism:** Something happens which represents an immediate improvement. For example, a customer telling a bank teller that they're unhappy with low interest rates, enabling the teller to provide a brochure about the bank's higher-yielding products.
- ▪ **Conformist Innovation**: This is Uber, which is a taxi service on steroids. But for smaller businesses, it's to have a superior delivery service, an online chat option, or evening hours. Several dry cleaners here pick up and deliver as does my car detail place. Pet grooming vans now visit homes.
- ▪ **Non-Conformist Innovation:** Amazon is the 2,000-pound gorilla here (it began as a book distributor), but for smaller businesses this is the "day spa" where dozens of services are available without traveling far from home of spending overnight visits. Telehealth is another, whereby medical costs are reduced and patients receive faster answers and more effective treatment than they would waiting for office visits.

Leading through change involves continuous learning and adaptation. It helps teams to develop new skills and expertise that contribute to personal and organizational growth. How many people do math in their heads today when a calculator is almost always nearby? Most people who wear expensive watches do so as an accessory, not because they're required to tell the time! We've learned to use GPS while driving or walking, and we schedule Uber drivers in advance.

Businesses have learned to use technology in place of people for mundane tasks and to focus advertising on their most important demographic targets.

Effective change leadership demonstrates strong character qualities. It inspires confidence and trust among team members and stakeholders. People in organizations—whether 50 employees or 50,000—don't believe what they read or what they hear. *They only believe what they see.*

Consequently, how leaders act in situations that are rewarding, threatening, uncertain, unstable, conflicting, and so forth will provide the basis for how all employees act. "Do as I say, not as I do" has never been an effective leadership principle. People aren't necessarily looking for instant solutions or magical answers, but they are seeking the confidence that the journey will be safe.

It's a myth that people fear change. The outcome of the change usually looks appealing and desirous. *It's the uncertainty of the journey that stresses them.* Leaders of high character during periods of change have to demonstrate that they may not have all the answers, but they do know a safe path on which everyone will be safe.

In Figure 9.1, you'll see that the key is the journey through ambiguity, not necessarily "solutions" and "answers."

By embracing and leading change, business leaders can streamline processes, improve efficiency, and optimize overall performance, even during challenging times. Historically, these organizations were founded during depressions, recessions, and general economic downturns:

- GE
- IBM
- Hewlett Packard
- Trader Joe's

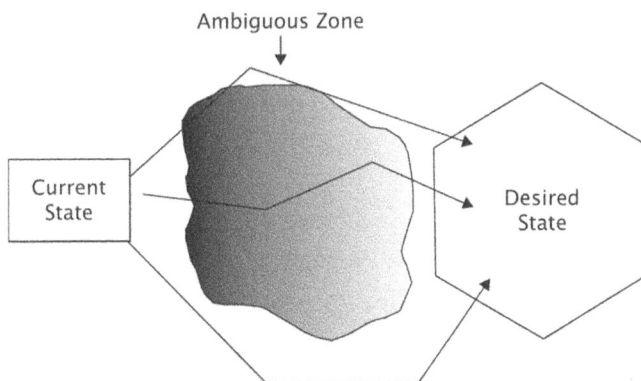

Figure 9.1   Transiting the ambiguous zone.

Source: **The Consulting Bible**, *Alan Weiss, Wiley, 2021.*

- Microsoft
- GM
- Disney
- Hyatt Hotels
- FedEx
- Electronic Arts

In addition, Salesforce, Google, and Facebook were all launched and prospered through significant economic troubles.

Even during the height of the pandemic, some businesses and markets were begun and thrived:

- Remote work platforms, such as Zoom
- Telehealth
- Do-it-yourself (DIY) home improvements
- Alcohol sales
- Supermarket foods
- Delivery services
- Fitness equipment
- Online gaming and gambling
- Streaming services
- Pet supplies

Note how many of these that embraced change were small businesses—from liquor stores to gyms.

Organizations that are adept at navigating change are more likely to achieve long-term success, as they can adapt to evolving market demands and challenges. Once leaders learn the process, they become better and better navigators of change.

Learning From Failure

Analyzing failures enhances decision-making skills by highlighting what doesn't work and that helps to refine future strategies. We learn from defeats more than victories. The point of resilience is to bounce forward from defeat.

Learning from failure teaches adaptability, which is an essential skill for navigating the rapidly changing world of business. The ability to adjust plans and recreate journeys is of the utmost importance.

Reflecting on failures and managing the associated emotions boosts emotional intelligence, which aids in better leadership and team dynamics. These are the traits of emotional intelligence which leaders should be helping individuals and teams adopt, so as to improve productivity and collaboration:

- Be more self-aware.
- Recognize how others feel.
- Practice active listening.
- Communicate clearly.
- Stay positive.
- Empathize.
- Be open-minded.
- Listen to feedback.

Shared experiences of failure and learning can strengthen team bonds. They foster a culture of support and collective growth. Leaders and followers have to build up experiences that help them become familiar with the warning signs of failure before they go over the edge of the cliff. Giants such as Sears and GE weren't sufficiently adept at this, and such blindness accounts for the staggering rate of small business failures within the first five years of business.[3]

Regularly learning from failure diminishes the fear of making mistakes. It encourages more risk-taking and creativity in business strategies.

> *Success is never final and failure seldom fatal—*
> *it's courage that counts.*
>
> —Winston Churchill

Each failure provides valuable lessons that can guide future actions and strategies. Failure turns potential pitfalls into stepping stones for success. Some failure constitutes success in other areas. Everything from crazy glue to Velcro was a result of the failure of the original intent of the developers.

Fostering a Growth Mindset with Your Teams

A growth-oriented culture promotes open communication and collaboration. Team members are more likely to share knowledge and learn from each other. One of the greatest expenses in business is poor team coordination and mutual support, which often results in duplication of effort, and much more expense acquiring new business and sustaining existing business than is necessary.

Teams that embrace a growth mindset approach problems with curiosity and an eagerness to find solutions. This can improve their problem-solving capabilities as well as their innovation on a daily basis. For businesses to succeed longer-term they must grow, and to continually grow they must innovate. Innovation is best promoted when that original growth mindset is present.

A workplace that values learning and development fosters higher levels of engagement. It makes employees feel their growth is supported and valued. Those employees, in turn, act as "ambassadors" to bring more talent to the firm because of the benefits of such development. Thus, acquisition costs for hiring are severely reduced and involuntary turnover can be reduced to virtually zero.

A growth mindset not only benefits the team as a whole, but also supports the personal development of each member. It aligns individual growth with organizational goals. This is a chronic problem in many organizations because succession planning, which is dictated by the senior management, doesn't always mesh with career development, which is often the province of human resources or learning and development. It's important that every individual receives the training and coaching appropriate for his or her future in the company's strategy and expectations.

As team members overcome challenges and develop new skills, their confidence grows. This leads to a more empowered and proactive team, one that requires less daily management, one that is self-motivated, and one that serves as a role model for others.

Notes

1 "I've always reflected that the success or failure of people are a matter of suiting their conduct to the times."—Machiavelli (*The Prince*)
2 www.census.gov/retail/mrts/www/data/pdf/ec_current.pdf
3 According to the U.S. Bureau of Labor Statistics (BLS), approximately 20% of new businesses fail during the first two years of being open, 45% during the first five years, and 65% during the first 10 years. Only 25% of new businesses make it to 15 years or more.

Chapter 10

Planning for the Future with Optimism

Cultivating an Optimistic Mindset

Start or end your day by listing things for which you're grateful. Gratitude shifts your focus from what's lacking to what's abundant in your life, fostering optimism. Too often we arise with negative thoughts, fears of what might occur, and depression about what we'll have to do (follow up on overdue invoices, deal with unhappy customers).

First, be thankful for things that you treasure: family, pets, health, success, and so forth. Don't fret because things aren't "perfect." No car, dinner, vacation, or house has ever been perfect. We simply make the most out of them that we can—and that's how we should try to structure our day.

Keep your goals reasonable and achievable. Break your future plans into small, manageable goals (as we discussed with organizing time and setting priorities earlier). Achieving these goals can boost your confidence and reinforce a positive outlook towards bigger challenges.

Small wins build larger successes. Success is incremental. Most sales are really a series of "small yesses":

- Yes, I believe our employees are our greatest asset.
- Yes, I believe in investing in their development.

DOI: 10.4324/9781003616597-11

- Yes, I think we need fresh interventions from the outside.
- Yes, I'd consider a proposal from you.
- Yes, we'll proceed with your services.[1]

This is the same phenomenon as innovation: A succession of incremental improvements leads to substantial improvement. Help your employees create small wins: One new client, one additional service, one complaint reversed into an "upsell." When teams are substantially behind their opponents, those most likely to come back are hearing their coach urge, "One touchdown (or goal, or run) at a time. Just start with the first one."

There's no such thing as a "minor victory." Small victories create the momentum and belief that enable larger things to follow. Tom Brady and the New England Patriots recovered from a 25-point deficit to beat the Atlanta Falcons in overtime at the Super Bowl. They did it one score at a time.

Surround yourself with positivity. Spend time with people who uplift you and avoid those who drain your energy. Positive social interactions can enhance your optimism. Don't go to meetings just because you were invited or because of your position. Ask if you're really needed there and refuse if meetings are simply a means of sharing information which could easily be shared by email.

Create a workspace that's uplifting. Use art, photos, and mementos that recall positive family and professional moments. (People who work remotely often have this without even planning.) Try to have natural light. Don't go so far as to not have chairs in your office for visitors, but discourage people from dropping in to complain, or object, or bemoan their fate.

Conversely, limit negative reminders and inputs. Reduce exposure to negative news, social media, or any content that can affect your mood and well-being. Instead, seek out inspiring and uplifting stories. Remember that the media thrive on sensationalism and catastrophism, not "good news" stories, so don't feel obligated to stay up-to-date during the day. If there's a true catastrophe, you'll hear about it soon enough.

In other words, control your environment; don't let it unthinkingly control you.

You'll need a growth mindset. View challenges as opportunities to learn and grow, rather than insurmountable obstacles. This mindset encourages resilience and optimism. We've talked about resilience. And we've talked about the ability to learn from failure and setbacks. Growth is about analyzing all experiences in order to learn and improve, not to make excuses or to find someone to blame.

Plateaus don't create success; they eventually erode (the laws of entropy). To survive, you have to grow, and to grow, you have to innovate. Innovation involves prudent risk and occasional failure. Focus on the longer-term growth not the immediate failure.

PERSEVERANCE PRESSURE

What you believe creates attitudes which are manifest in your behaviors. If you truly believe in growth and have that mindset, then you act that way as an exemplar and create actions to sustain it.

Spend time visualizing your goals and the positive outcomes of your efforts. Visualization can create a mental blueprint, making your goals feel more attainable. Familiarity makes speakers more comfortable on stage, which is why professionals go on the stage well before their event. Familiarity with a client's office creates a more comfortable sales setting.

Even when you can't become familiar with a certain goal or task, think about it—what it might look like, who might be there, what the dynamics may be. With unpleasant situations, perhaps a complaining customer or unhappy employee, the situation is often not as bad as you had feared or prepared for.

Engage in mindfulness[2] practices like meditation or deep breathing exercises. Being present can reduce stress and promote a more positive outlook. Stop preparing a response or objection or additional comment, and just *listen*—not just to the words but to the intent of the message.

That will help in reframing negative thoughts. Actively challenge and reframe negative thoughts into more positive, realistic ones. This cognitive restructuring can help build an optimistic mindset. An objection is a sign of interest (apathy is the real threat). Disagreement means there is passion.

Recognize and celebrate your achievements, *no matter how small*. This reinforces the belief that progress is being made, fueling further optimism. We've discussed this earlier, referring to small victories.

Finally, regular exercise, a balanced diet, and adequate sleep can significantly impact your mental health—boosting mood and fostering an optimistic outlook. Your physical, emotional, and mental well-being are all closely intertwined.[3]

Takeaway

Cultivating an optimistic mindset is not about ignoring life's challenges but about approaching them with a positive, proactive attitude.

By integrating these practices into your daily life, you can build a foundation of optimism that supports your future plans and aspirations (and can inspire your people).

Strategic Vision and Goal-Setting

Define your vision: Start with a clear and compelling vision that outlines what you want to achieve (and "look like") in the future. This vision should inspire and motivate you, employees, customers, and other stakeholders— serving as a North Star for your actions and decisions.

Don't confuse "vision" with "mission." The latter is why you exist; the former is the manifestation or "proof" of your success in your mission.

If your mission is to "Provide safety and comfort in visiting global destinations for learning and enjoyment," then the vision might be that you're constantly in receipt of unsolicited referrals to arrange trips for individuals and groups.

This means that you must honestly evaluate where you are in relation to your mission and vision. Understanding your starting point is crucial for setting realistic and achievable goals. What are the metrics that are in place for all to see and experience? They may be, in this example:

- Unsolicited referrals weekly.
- Over 50% of customers are repeat customers.
- You are written about favorably in industry publications.
- Your credit score is high.
- You have small involuntary turnover.
- Your technology is state-of-the-art.

The time to measure your success *is while you're doing business, not at some random point of year-end review.*

Ensure your goals are SMART: Specific, Measurable, Achievable, Relevant, and Time-bound. SMART goals provide clarity and direction, making it easier to focus your efforts and track progress. If you can't measure it, you're probably not going to achieve it. You can't "guess" at progress.

Divide each goal into smaller, manageable tasks. This approach makes it less overwhelming to start and maintain momentum towards achieving your larger goals. This is similar to our earlier discussion about priorities. Not all goals are created equal. Prioritize them based on their relevance to your vision and the impact they will have. Focus on what truly matters to make the most significant progress. Remember *seriousness, urgency, and growth*:

▪ How **serious** (positive, opportunistic) is the issue?
▪ How **important** is rapid action (urgency)?
▪ If we don't act, will we lose the opportunity, or will it remain (**growth**)?

Establish a realistic timeline for each goal and task. Deadlines create a sense of urgency and help you manage your time more effectively. Ideally, a spreadsheet that can be accessed and updated by all relevant parties and stakeholders is a great mechanism to check progress in real time. This can account for decisions to change priorities and tactics.

For example, are your resources being allocated intelligently according to your priorities, or do they need to be redeployed? Identify the resources (time, money, skills, support) that you need for each goal and plan how to allocate them most efficiently. This preparation prevents resource constraints from derailing your plans. It will also encourage more proactive resource sharing to make sure everyone "wins" and prevents you from having to spend time doing this yourself.

Regularly review your progress towards your goals and adjust as needed. Be prepared to adjust your plans as needed in response to feedback and changing circumstances. While having a strategic vision and goals is important, staying flexible and open to new opportunities is equally crucial. Sometimes, unexpected paths may lead to fulfilling your vision in ways you hadn't imagined. You have to be sensitive to expected *or unexpected* changes in the market, customer base, technology, social mores, government regulations, competition, and so forth.

Celebrate milestones. Acknowledge and celebrate when you reach important progress indicators. This not only boosts morale but also reinforces the connection between effort and achievement, keeping you motivated towards your larger vision. Hence, when you've "chunked" things into smaller parts, you'll have more milestones to reach to generate more momentum and small "wins."

Takeaway

Strategic vision and goal-setting transforms optimism into actionable plans. By following these steps, you can create a roadmap that guides your actions and decisions, moving you confidently towards your desired future, which may change as you move forward, and for which you can adapt and seize more opportunity.

Investing in People and Relationships

Open, honest, and consistent communication builds trust and understanding. Make it a priority to regularly check in with your colleagues, friends, and family. There are plenty of formal opportunities for communication: meetings, joint projects, memos, announcements, and so forth. But make it a point to have casual communications: chats in the hall, shared meals, impromptu requests for advice. If you do this continually, people will not be shocked or afraid when they are asked!

Regularly express gratitude to those around you. Acknowledging others' efforts and contributions fosters positive relationships and mutual respect. The literature of the last decade proves that money is not a motivator. If you give an unhappy employee more money, you have a wealthier, unhappy employee. What *does* allow people to become motivated is recognition of their work and the freedom to fail.[4]

Quality time is one of the most significant investments you can make in any relationship. Dedicate time to listen, support, and engage with people genuinely. And offer discretionary time: Allow people to set their own schedules and, if possible, allow for at least some remote work. Many employees feel that this kind of freedom is often worth more than small financial incentives, and can remedy the problems arising from child-care issues, traffic problems, and even mild illnesses.

Strive to understand others' perspectives and feelings. Empathy strengthens connections and builds a supportive network, crucial for future challenges and opportunities. Empathy, don't forget, is "feeling what the other person feels" (as opposed to "sympathy" which is feeling sorry for another person's plight).

- *Emotional Empathy* is understanding what the other person needs.
- *Intellectual Empathy* is recognizing that need.
- *Experiential Empathy* is identifying with that need.

Helping people, from simple advice to active support, requires trust and the manifestation of empathy.

If you have the first two, but not the third, you won't have the ability to have "been there and done that" to use for your support (a divorce, being fired, losing a major client, perhaps). If you have the bottom two but not the first, then you won't be able to make a connection with this person, even though you've been through it yourself. And if you have the other two but lack the middle factor, you won't even know that your assistance is needed.

Empathy is required for coaching and mentoring others towards growth. Support the personal and professional growth of those around you. Encouragement can boost confidence and motivation, benefiting both the individual and the collective. Organizations (and individuals) can't survive, let alone thrive, without growth, and growth can't take place without innovation. You can see this in Figure 10.1, the "S-curve."

After a new venture (or product or service) is introduced and is successful, it gains momentum until growth inevitably slows and a plateau appears. This is the "success trap" because *all plateaus eventually erode.* Consequently, the time to "leap" to the next S-curve is when you have maximum momentum and acceleration and the leap is easiest, as indicated by the X on the chart. If you wait to leap until you're far along on the plateau, you'll have little momentum and a far greater distance to jump.

To create this kind of mentality and environment, you need to foster a culture where positivity, respect, and kindness prevail. A positive atmosphere enhances collaboration and creativity. You are the exemplar for this—not human resources, not memos or plaques on the walls. "We respect our people (customers, etc.)" is easy to write but harder to exemplify. Employees don't necessarily believe what they read or hear, they believe *what they observe.*

Create a network of support, comprising family, friends, and professional contacts. This network will be invaluable during both good times and challenges. Some people call it an "advisory board" but, essentially, what you need is a small group of people to whom you can talk candidly, in a

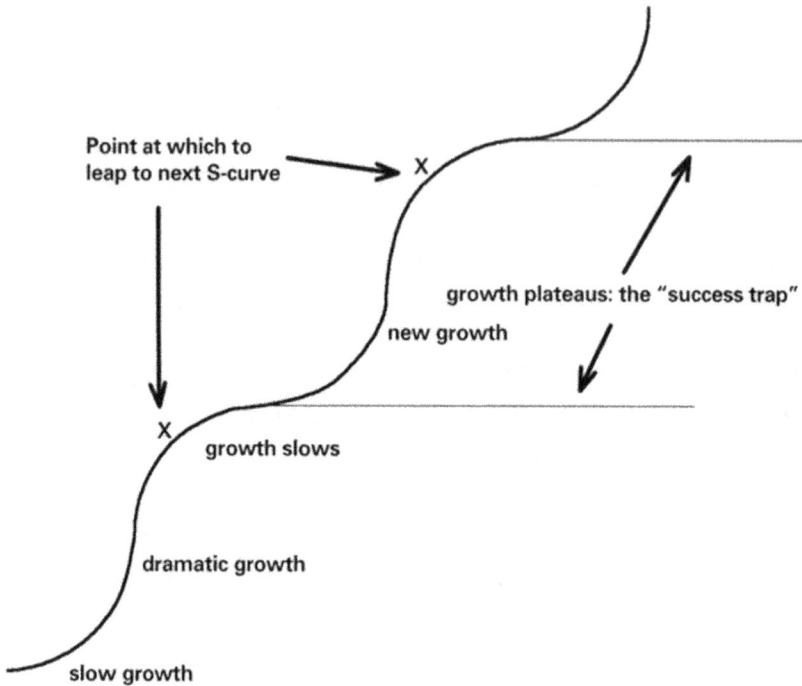

Figure 10.1 The S-curve.

Source: Sentient Strategy, *Alan Weiss, Routledge, 2024.*

group or individually, to gain feedback on the challenges that arise and on the responses you've made or are considering. Your self-esteem should be constantly high, not as low as your last defeat or as high as your last victory.

This group is especially important because solicited feedback from those you trust is always helpful. Unsolicited feedback is not, because it's for the sender, not for you. That's why you should seek feedback from customers and clients, not just sit back and listen to what is provided.

Thus, listen to understand, not just to respond. Active listening shows that you value others' thoughts and feelings, deepening your relationships. Use "tests for understanding." If someone tells you that they agree with you, *ask how they would use or apply your point.* That ensures they've understood to the extent of actual application and aren't just trying to make you happy!

Resolve conflicts constructively: Address misunderstandings and disagreements openly and positively. Resolving issues promptly prevents them from undermining relationships. Seek compromise and "win/win/win" (customer, employee, you, for example). This might require compromise, consensus, or a third or fourth option entirely.

Then you can celebrate success together. Share and celebrate successes with your team, friends, and family. Celebrating together strengthens bonds and creates shared memories. And this helps you overcome the setbacks and the inevitable mistakes.

Takeaway

Investing in people and relationships lays a strong foundation for a hopeful and optimistic future. These investments yield returns in the form of support, collaboration, and shared joy, which are invaluable as you navigate the path ahead.

Measuring Success and Staying Accountable

Define what success looks like for each goal. Clear benchmarks make it easier to measure progress and know when you've achieved your objectives. These are "metrics" or "measures of progress."

Zeno's Paradox states that "If you make half the distance toward your goal every day, you'll never reach it." Thus, you need measures of success *and measures of completion.* A simple spreadsheet can help you track who is responsible for what results at what points. This kind of attentiveness will:

■ Prevent people from failing to meet accountabilities by claiming confusion or miscommunication.
■ Identify who may need help at what points.
■ Correct poor progress before it endangers the overall deadline.
■ Assign the right talent to the right needs.
■ Celebrate victory upon completion.

People often tend to do the easiest or the quickest and claim progress, but if their accomplishments don't meet the metrics and timeframes, then they're illusory and deceptive. You don't win a baseball game because you have a better score after the sixth inning; you need the better score at the end of the game.

We're often "lulled" into an assumption of progress because early, easy goals are met but tougher ones are placed on hold. If we're honest about metrics, *we can learn from our mistakes.* The manager who is behind every quarter but says it will be "made up" by the end of the year will eventually tell you after failing to meet goals at year-end, "They were unfair goals, I tried my best."

We can't afford this kind of poor performance and/or duplicity.

Use Key Performance Indicators (KPIs): Identify specific, quantifiable indicators related to your goals. KPIs provide a measurable way to track progress and assess performance over time. For example:

- Minimum of three repair calls a day.
- Acquisition of five referrals a week.
- Preventive maintenance performed/documented every Friday.
- All calls returned within 90 minutes during business hours.
- Customer "hold" time is less than three minutes.
- Website "specials" updated every Monday morning.
- Driver schedules distributed Friday by 3 pm for coming week.

It's helpful to have the people involved contribute to these KPIs, so that they don't feel these expectations are "imposed" on them, but are realistic and reasonable. Performance evaluations should be based on KPIs, and KPIs should change in changing circumstances:

- Supply chain problems
- New technology
- New products/services
- Customer complaints

One of the reasons that we're receiving so many surveys today—from hotels, online products purchased, restaurants, pet stores, and so forth—is that the organizations want to ensure their KPIs are accurate, pleasing customers, and consistently met.

Schedule periodic reviews to assess your progress towards goals. These reviews allow you to celebrate achievements, reflect on challenges, and adjust strategies as needed. These are great opportunities to involve others, delegate, and create collaboration and consensus on the progress and any corrections that need to be made. It's said by some that "if you can't measure it, it's not important," but you can add to that "if you don't heed the measures, it's not important."

The key to such reviews is to create momentum and positivity, not to create blame and find fault.

Reviews can include clients (see the "surveys" discussed above) and other stakeholders, such as suppliers, town officials, civic groups, and investors/bankers. You're under no obligation to act on everything you're told or on "one-off" feedback, but if you detect patterns among disparate feedback then the chances are you should pay attention and make necessary changes.

We know of one firm, for example, that produced an inferior product and assumed it knew the cause. Correcting that "cause" enabled it to send two products out for each one returned, so that they were providing customers with an apology and bonus. The difficulty here was that the company had the *wrong cause,* so it was sending out *two inferior* products for every single one returned!

Maintain a progress journal in order to keep a detailed record of your actions, results, and reflections. A progress journal is a powerful tool for self-accountability and learning from your experiences. It allows you to avoid creating past mistakes but also to ensure you replicate past successes.

Does your sales team, or call center, or operations staff have a history of varied results, where some people outperform others? Don't just assume it's skill (or luck), but investigate whether they all are aware of and have access to the best practices of the moment. A progress journal will enable you to "share the information wealth" and attempt to bring all performers up to the highest levels.

Make your goals known to a trusted friend, mentor, or peer group. Sharing your goals creates a sense of commitment and can provide you with a support network for accountability. This is the "public accountability" that we all need. Whether family, friends, memberships, or stakeholders, when people know their goals are known to others who are interested in their progress, they tend to make faster, better progress in meeting those goals.

Third parties have far less understanding in excuses and defensiveness, and often have good ideas—when you are honest about your lack of progress—about how to overcome obstacles and regain momentum toward your goals. Tuck your ego away and consider such "public disclosure" the best pathway toward success.

Thus, actively seek and be open to feedback. Constructive feedback is invaluable for personal growth and for making necessary adjustments to your approach. *Feedback you seek from those whom you respect—solicited feedback—is always valuable and can be trusted. But unsolicited feedback— from people whom you did not ask—is normally for the sender's ego and not your benefit.* Feel safe to say, "thank you" and then ignore it. Otherwise, you'll become a ping pong ball.

If you want more personal and intimate feedback, partner with someone who is also looking to achieve his or her own goals. Mutual accountability can significantly increase your motivation and commitment. A team moving forward can be highly effective when there is trust, reciprocity, and a win/win mentality.

View setbacks as learning opportunities rather than failures. Analyzing what went wrong and why can provide insights that help you adjust your approach and avoid similar issues in the future. *Every interaction*, no matter what the outcome, should be a learning opportunity. If not, then besides the setback, you've wasted time and haven't learned how to deal with the issue the next time.

Takeaway

Measuring success and staying accountable are about setting clear goals, tracking your progress, and being willing to learn and adjust along the way. By embracing these practices, you can navigate your path with confidence and optimism, knowing that you are actively working towards your desired future.

The practices in this chapter will enable you not only to effectively plan your future, but to do so optimistically. And I hope this book has provided you with the perseverance to triumph in challenging and changing times, which should be what we look forward to and not fear.

Notes

1 Psychologically, in terms of influence, this is called consistency.
2 A mental state achieved by focusing one's awareness on the present moment, while calmly acknowledging and accepting one's feelings, thoughts, and bodily sensations, often called "being in the moment" and sometimes used as a therapeutic technique.
3 www.health.com/weekend-warrior-exercise-brain-health-8704302
4 www.gallup.com/workplace/236441/employee-recognition-low-cost-high-imp act.aspx#:~:text=Workplace%20recognition%20motivates%2C%20provides%20 a,company%2C%20leading%20to%20higher%20retention

Index

Note: Page numbers in *italics* indicate figures on the corresponding pages.

For Product Safety Concerns and Information please contact our EU
representative GPSR@taylorandfrancis.com
Taylor & Francis Verlag GmbH, Kaufingerstraße 24, 80331 München, Germany

www.ingramcontent.com/pod-product-compliance
Lightning Source LLC
Chambersburg PA
CBHW080559220326
41599CB00032B/6540

9 781041 018438